Wines and Wineries of the
Barossa Valley

# Wines and Wineries of the Barossa Valley

Bryce Rankine

The Jacaranda Press

First published 1971 by
JACARANDA PRESS PTY LTD
46 Douglas Street, Milton, Q.
32 Church Street, Ryde, N.S.W.
37 Little Bourke Street, Melbourne, Vic.
142 Colin Street, West Perth, W.A.
298a Grange Road, Flinders Park, S.A.
57 France Street, Auckland, N.Z.
P.O. Box 3395, Port Moresby, P.N.G.
122 Regents Park Road, London NW1

Typesetting by Watson Ferguson & Company, Brisbane
Printed in Hong Kong

© Bryce Rankine 1971

National Library of Australia
Card Number and ISBN 0 7016 0513 8

All rights reserved. No part of this publication may be reproduced, stored in a retrieval system, or transmitted in any form or by any means, electronic, mechanical, photocopying, recording, or otherwise, without the prior permission of the publisher.

To the Winemakers of the
Barossa Valley

Back of this Wine is the Vintner,
And back through the years his Skill
And back of it all are the Vines in the Sun
And the Rain, and the Master's Will.

# Contents

|    | Preface                                    | ix |
|----|--------------------------------------------|----|
| 1  | The Barossa Valley                         | 1  |
| 2  | Seppelt's and Seppeltsfield                | 7  |
| 3  | Gramp's Orlando                            | 12 |
| 4  | Yalumba                                    | 19 |
| 5  | Penfolds and Port                          | 24 |
| 6  | Saltram of Angaston                        | 28 |
| 7  | Henschke and the Hill of Grace             | 31 |
| 8  | Kaiser Stuhl                               | 34 |
| 9  | Tolley, Scott & Tolley                     | 39 |
| 10 | Château Leonay                             | 41 |
| 11 | Basedow's Wines                            | 45 |
| 12 | Hoffmann's of North Para                   | 46 |
| 13 | St Hallett's Wines                         | 47 |
| 14 | Glen View and Matara                       | 49 |
| 15 | Hardy's Siegersdorf                        | 50 |
| 16 | Rovalley Wines                             | 52 |
| 17 | Château Yaldara                            | 53 |
| 18 | Wilsford Wines                             | 56 |
| 19 | Château Rosevale                           | 57 |
| 20 | Hamilton's of Springton and Eden Valley    | 58 |
| 21 | The Barossa Valley Vintage Festival        | 60 |
| 22 | Miscellany                                 | 63 |

23 Wine Types    66
24 Technical Talk: *Fermentation,
   Winemaking processes, Flor Sherry*    73
25 Grapes in the Barossa    85
26 Climate of the Barossa    90
27 Soils of the Barossa    96
28 Grape and Wine Research in the Barossa    98
29 The Future    102
   Map    104
   Index    105

# Preface

FINE wines are made in many parts of Australia, in areas extending from the Hunter River Valley in New South Wales to the Swan River Valley in Western Australia, a distance of nearly 2500 miles. Many other individual regions have developed reputations for wines of high quality; these include Rutherglen and nearby areas, Tahbilk and Great Western in Victoria, and the Barossa Valley, Clare and Watervale, Adelaide, Southern Vales, Coonawarra and Padthaway in South Australia. The irrigation areas of the River Murray and the Riverina are now making their own quality contribution and other areas are being developed.

This book is concerned with just one of these regions—the Barossa Valley and its adjacent Barossa Hills, including Eden Valley and Springton. The Barossa Valley is a magical name in the Australian wine industry. It is the home of some of the finest wines in Australia, and some of the largest and best-equipped wineries. Traditionally, the Barossa was synonymous with fine dessert wines and brandy, with some table wines thrown in—but no longer. With the increasing demand for table wines by discriminating Australian wine drinkers, the Barossa wineries have shown that they can produce white and red table wines of a quality as fine as the dessert wines which first brought them fame. The Barossa Valley has other charms as well—fine people, attractive scenery and a unique history.

I have endeavoured to present the background to Barossa wines—the winemakers and wineries, their history, their wines—and also some general technical background to explain why wines are made as they are, and what goes on in the remarkable process called fermentation.

In writing this account of the Barossa Valley and its wines, I have had to be selective. There are so many wines which ought to be mentioned that I have had to pick and choose. To do this without offence is certainly difficult, and perhaps impossible. What does the Barossa Valley mean to a wine-lover? Perhaps tasting fragrant Rieslings at Orlando, or fine sherries with Rudi Kronberger in the cool Yalumba cellars or at Seppelsfield, or fine reds at Château Leonay with John Vickery, or ports with Ray Beckwith of Penfolds, or sparkling wines among the art treasures of Château Yaldara. Perhaps all these things and many more. But to write about Barossa wines to encompass all these things . . .

Selectivity is necessary for another reason. Not all wines made in the Barossa come from Barossa grapes. Are these therefore Barossa wines? Many grapes come to the Barossa Valley each year from other areas—from vineyards on the River Murray, from Clare, Watervale and elsewhere. I have tried to be selective without being too restrictive.

Many people have helped, directly or indirectly, with this book. I am indebted to Bob and Ian Seppelt, Ray Beckwith, Colin Gramp, Guenther Prass, Oscar Semmler, George Kolarovich, Wyndham Hill-Smith, Rudi Kronberger, Alfred Wark, Peter Lehmann, Cyril Henschke, Reg Shipster, John Vickery, John Basedow, 'Bart' Hebart, Bruce Hoffmann, Bill and Elmore Lindner, Jim Irvine, 'Darkie' Liebich, Lance Ackland, Bob Wade, Phil Tummel, Wolfgang Blass, Noel Burge, Robert Hamilton, Ron Burton and many others. They are fine people and their help is greatly appreciated. I hope that I have done justice to them and their wines.

My thanks go particularly to Jack Ludbrook, George Fairbrother and Wally Boehm, and also to Professor J. A. Prescott, Don Redman, Keith Northcote, Albert Whitelaw and my daughter Jenny Rankine. I acknowledge also the kindly help of Jack Ludbrook (again), the Wine Information Bureau, the Australian Wine Board, Wolfgang Sievers of Melbourne, Lawrence Rhodes of Adelaide, and wineries in the Valley for providing many of the photographs. I am particularly grateful to my wife, Ellaine for typing the manuscript and for her many constructive comments. Writing this book has been an interesting and enjoyable task, and I hope that those who read it will find it of interest.

Bryce Rankine
February 1971

# 1
# The Barossa Valley

IN the hot South Australian summers, when the land assumes a sunburnt brown appearance, the Barossa is a welcome and refreshing sight, with its vast acres of green vines extending in orderly rows. The Valley starts near Williamstown, south of Lyndoch, about thirty five miles from Adelaide, and extends twenty miles north-east through Tanunda and Nuriootpa to end at St Kitt's Hills. Its width varies from two to seven miles. From the air, the Valley has an area rather like the silhouette of a bottle lying on its side with the neck towards Williamstown—a pertinent analogy!

In geological language, the Valley is a tectonic fault, an earth movement in which a portion of the land's surface slipped vertically downwards in the distant past, forming a flat depression with the eastern side against the Barossa Hills, which are part of the Mount Lofty Ranges. The North Para River meanders south-west through the Valley to join the South Para River at Gawler; here the confluence forms the Gawler River, running westward to enter St Vincent's Gulf at Port Gawler.

In discussing the wines of the Barossa Valley, one must also consider the Eden Valley-Springton area in the Barossa Hills as part of the same region. Some of the finest Barossa wines come from the Eden Valley and the eastern foothills of the Barossa Valley.

There is some confusion over the name of the Valley.

Correctly, the name is 'Barrosa' (Hill of Roses), so named by Colonel William Light after a ridge in southern Spain commanding the entrance to the Bermeja Peninsula, which carries the road to Cadiz. The name was misspelled on an early map by a draughtsman, and the error has been allowed to stand. Historically, therefore, the hills are Barrosa and the Valley at its southern extremity is Lynedoch Vale (again misspelled), named by Light in 1837 after Lord Lynedoch, who was at one time Light's commanding officer and who fought in the victorious battle against the French at the Barrosa in 1811.

The first inhabitants of the Barossa were the Aborigines, who led a simple nomadic life, wandering from place to place in search of food. They were few in number and soon disappeared on the arrival of the white settlers, who showed little interest in them. The Aborigines knew nothing of viticulture and wine, and indeed, could have known nothing, since there were no grapes in Australia. (The only representative of the grapevine family, *Vitis*, was in Northern Australia and did not produce edible fruit.) The first colonists in South Australia arrived in July 1836, and the Province was proclaimed at Glenelg by Governor Hindmarsh on 28 December of that year. It was not until December of the following year that the first white men (Colonel Light and his party) entered the Valley. They were seeking a north-eastern route to the River Murray, but on arrival at the 'Tanunda Creek', they turned back. It was on this trip that Lyndoch (Lynedoch) was named (13 December, 1837).

Soon other men followed. One of these was a German geologist and mineralogist named Johann Menge; his visit had been arranged by George Fife Angas, who became known as the Father of the Barossa Valley. Johann Menge's report stated: 'I am certain that we shall see the place flourish, and vineyards and orchards and immense fields of corn throughout. It will furnish huge quantities of wine; it will yield timber for our towns, and superior stone and marble abounds for buildings.' Johann Menge's vision for the Barossa was as vivid as Colonel William Light's vision for Adelaide: both have been fulfilled.

The path of the first settlers lay along the valley surveyed by Rowland (after whom Rowland Flat was named), and the track blazed by Colonel Light in 1837. It forked at a point where Nuriootpa now stands (named Angas Park by Charles Flaxman), leading thence to a peak of the ranges in a line from Angas Park to Penrice. Crossing the hill, this path led south-east down to the valley that later was to contain Angas Town or Angaston, surveyed in 1841. This town was named after George Fife Angas, born in Newcastle, England, in 1789, who established the South Australian Company to settle the new colony. He was also largely responsible for the development of the valley, and it was he who arranged, with Pastor August Ludwig Christian Kavel, to bring out the first three boat-loads of German migrants from Silesia in 1838. The first German settlement of twenty-eight Lutheran families took place in 1842 at Bethany (sometimes referred to in early documents as Neuschlesien—new Silesia). Several years later, the settlement at Langmeil, from which Tanunda was to grow, was established a few miles away on the North Para River. (Tanunda is an Aboriginal name meaning 'water hole'.) Nuriootpa (again an Aboriginal word meaning 'meeting place') later grew as a staging camp on the way to the copper mines at Kapunda and Burra. It was laid out by William Coulthard in 1854. Colonization proceeded rapidly in the forties and fifties. Johann Gramp settled at Jacob's Creek and Samuel Hoffmann at Tanunda in 1847. Samuel Smith founded the Yalumba venture in 1849; Joseph Ernst Seppelt established himself at Seppeltsfield in 1851, and William Salter and his son Edward were planting vines near Angaston in 1859. The people who made the greatest contribution to the Valley were the German-speaking immigrants, but the Salters, the Smiths and others, gave the English colonists a share in the honours.

The German dialect sometimes heard in the Valley today is quaint and probably unique as an ethnic language. The Silesian dialect is still evident in pronunciation, although the language has become curiously modified in its 130 years of linguistic isolation—a combination of Silesian German and English, commonly known as 'Barossa Deutsch'. One way to learn about the Barossa is to visit the cemeteries! Many of the old tombstone inscriptions read *'Hier ruhet in Gott . . .'* (Here rests in God . . .) which refers back to the origin of the people half a world away. The German language is, regrettably, gradually dying out.

The Valley today presents many facets of German life and customs. Names on shops in Tanunda, Nuriootpa, Angaston and elsewhere frequently record the German origin of their owners, and picturesque, neatly maintained Lutheran churches dot the landscape. On the farms one may still find the typical German wagons, with their large wheels and sloping sides. These ubiquitous wagons once served as all forms of transport—family coach, hay cart, heavy transport, caravan, grape carrier, water cart, hearse and wedding chaise. It was impossible to find a family without one. The immigrants brought with them their traditional foods—Streuselkuchen (crumble-top cake), Honigkuchen (honey biscuits), Quarkkuchen (cheese cake), Quark Stinkerkase (cottage cheese—and what an expressive name!) Sauerkraut (sour cabbage), Mettwurst, Blutwurst and Leberwurst (small goods). These are still sold in shops in the Valley. A slab of fresh Streuselkuchen, for example, is both delightful and typically Barossa.

The people have an inherited love for music. The German Tanunda Liedertafel is almost as old as the town itself. It is a choral society, which was established in 1861 and has continued without interruption ever since. Brass bands and annual band competitions are another feature of the Valley's musical life. Some of the little hamlets have strong historical associations—names like Langmeil, Tabor, Ebenezer, Gnadenfrei, Bethany, Gruenberg and many others appear in the very early records. Unfortunately, during the First World War, many of the German place names in the Valley were changed by Act of Parliament, and so a link with some of the early history was lost. These changes included Gnadenfrei (Marananga), Schoenborn (Gomersal), Krondorf (Kabminye), Siegersdorf (Dorrien), Kaiser-Stuhl (Mt Kitchener) and Langmeil (Bilyara). Happily, some of the original names were later restored.

Although religion is at the heart of local life, the occupational pattern of the Valley is woven in and around the vineyards. The Barossa has come to be synonymous with wine. Over 20,000 acres of vines are planted in the Valley and the Barossa Hills, and thirty wineries make wine in the Valley; it is the core of the wine industry in a state which produces two-thirds of Australia's wine.

Many of the German descendants have become wealthy men and leading citizens, and evidence of their work and influence can be seen in various aspects of life in the Valley. The Gramps, Seppelts and many others have enviable traditions in the wine industry of the Valley, and the neat and orderly rows of green leafy vines adorning the floor and slopes of the Valley are symbolic of something real, but less tangible—the thoroughness and dependability of the dwellers of the Valley.

The visitor may drive to the Valley from Adelaide by one of several routes. One of the most attractive ways is through the winding steep-sided Torrens Gorge, past the Kangaroo Creek and Milbrook reservoirs, turning north at Chain of Ponds to pass through Kersbrook and Williamstown, and entering the Valley at its beginning south of Lyndoch. This enables one to drive the full length of the Valley through Lyndoch, Rowland Flat, Tanunda, Dorrien (with a short side-trip to Seppeltsfield) and Nuriootpa, turning east to Angaston. From there, it is a short drive to the top of Mengler's Hill for a panoramic view of the valley; then one can return to Adelaide via Eden Valley, Springton,

Birdwood, Woodside, Aldgate and Stirling. This is a full-day trip of about 130 miles, enabling the visitor to see the Barossa and Eden Valleys and the location of many of the thirty wineries, as well as some fine scenery. A detour to the Barossa Reservoir near Williamstown, with its remarkable 'Whispering Wall', is well worthwhile if time permits.

There are of course shorter routes, but these are scenically less attractive. One may take the Main North Road through Elizabeth to Gawler, turning east to Sandy Creek and Lyndoch and thence northwards through the Valley, returning to Adelaide from Nuriootpa through Greenock, Daveyston, Shea Oak Log and on the bypass road around Gawler. The distance is about a hundred miles, but the roads are straighter and one can make the journey in a much shorter time.

# 2
# Seppelt's and Seppeltsfield

To any visitor to the Valley, Seppeltsfield is a 'must'. It is unlike any other winery in Australia, standing in majestic isolation on the western rim of the Valley in a fold in the hills. To many visitors, Seppeltsfield *is* the Barossa Valley; a recent count showed that nearly 50,000 visitors came to Seppeltsfield every year.

One reaches Seppeltsfield by turning west off the Sturt Highway at Dorrien, opposite 'Die Weinstube' restaurant, and driving past the Dorrien branch cellars of Seppelt's and over the low rolling hills that form the western wall of the Valley. On the way is the tiny hamlet of Marananga, with the picturesque little Lutheran church named Gnadenfrei, (the German influence is everywhere in the Valley). Then the road suddenly becomes lined with palm trees. This is Seppelt country. The palms are characteristic of all Seppelt's wineries.

The road enters a broad grove of Aleppo pines and, suddenly and dramatically, one is confronted with a piece of pure Ionic Greek architecture—the Seppelt Mausoleum. Designed by J. G. Seppelt, it is built on the highest land with a superb view of both Seppelt's and the Valley. If the visitor is not impressed by now, he is hard to please. The palms lead onwards until one arrives at Seppeltsfield, and it is like entering another world.

Seppeltsfield is actually a complex consisting of winery, maturation cellars, administrative offices, central laboratory, vinegar plant and distillery. It presents to the visitor an air of dignity, and gives the feeling that winemaking and maturation should not be a hurried business. The winery, built at the turn of the century, is one of the few in Australia to make use of gravity for movement of wine. The fermentation cellar was built on the slope of the hill and the open concrete fermentation tanks are arranged in stepped-down rows. Grapes enter at the top and are crushed and pumped to the tanks below. When the fermentation is completed, the wine is gravitated to storage vessels further down the hill. This unusual design harks back to the time when pumps for moving wine were operated by hand or by cumbersome and noisy motors. The introduction of electricity changed all this, but the winery remains as a distinctive feature of Seppeltsfield.

The central area of Seppeltsfield contains the laboratory and the adjacent administration offices. These, too, have striking architectural features. The laboratory is actually the quality control centre for the widespread Seppelt organization, and wines from the various other wineries (Château Tanunda, Dorrien, Great Western, Rutherglen and Griffith) are brought to the central laboratory for analysis and tasting. This laboratory was set up in the time of Les Francis and the late Mel Bell, both noted winemakers, and has been a tremendous asset to the far-flung Seppelt organization.

The various storage cellars at Seppeltsfield are used to mature wines made at the other wineries as well as at Seppeltsfield, and the quantity of oak storage is immense. One large cellar is devoted solely to maturing sherry on flor, whilst another is used only for maturation of port. The still-house walls are lined with awards gained from various wine shows in which B. Seppelt & Sons Ltd have been successful.

Part of the cellars has been reserved as an entertainment area for visitors, and a scale model of Seppeltsfield is set out to give an indication of the size and layout of the area. A new retail bottle shop was recently opened, offering special bottlings with individual labels. Nearby is a storage cellar filled with casks of old port. This is the Para Liqueur port, famous as one of the oldest and finest ports in Australia. The first such port to be sold was the 1923 vintage and, as time went by and the public became aware of what was being offered, stocks declined and 1939 is the vintage currently being offered. The wine is made from a blend of Shiraz, Mataro and Grenache grapes grown at Seppeltsfield. The name 'Para Liqueur' is taken from the North Para River, which runs through the Valley only four miles from Seppeltsfield.

Another Seppelt's winery in the Valley is Château Tanunda on the eastern outskirts of Tanunda. A large dignified old cellar with a 240 foot bluestone façade and a 64 foot tower, it was built by a previous owner in 1889. It is one of the outstanding châteaux of the Valley. As I write, Château Tanunda is undergoing a great change with the building of a new table wine processing area due east of the main building. Kevin Sobels the manager and Malcolm Seppelt, one of the sons of the company chairman and managing director Ian Seppelt O.B.E., are deeply involved with the new developments.

Behind a great organization like this there are usually great men. In the Seppelt family, one was particularly outstanding. His name was Benno, but let us start at the beginning.

Joseph Ernest Seppelt was born in Silesia in 1813 and became head of a family business making liqueurs, cordials and snuff at Wustewaltersdorf. He emigrated to Australia in September 1849 with his family, a group of employees and some other families from the area. They arrived in January 1850. He first settled at Golden Grove, then later at Klemzig, both now outer suburbs of Adelaide, and finally in 1851, near the town of Tanunda at a place which he called Seppeltsfield. Joseph first planted tobacco, but the climate proved unsuitable for this crop. Then he planted corn and established a small vineyard, the forerunner of the graceful contoured vineyards which surround Seppeltsfield today. He died in 1868 at the age of fifty-five.

Joseph's son Benno, at the age of twenty-one, took over the property. In the fifty years in which he was in charge of the enterprise, his achievements were monumental. By the time he retired in 1916, the Seppeltsfield vineyards, cellar and distillery were the show place they are today. He had also established interstate branches and bought a vineyard and winery at Rutherglen in Victoria. Château Tanunda was purchased in the year of his retirement. He developed the family enterprise to a point which even his father could scarcely have dreamed of. He is recorded as being hardworking and abstemious, thoughtful, inventive and extraordinarily thorough. His record of achievement speaks for itself, for by the time he died in 1930, at the age of eighty-five, the name of Seppelt was synonymous with winemaking throughout Australia. Benno was supported by a wonderful wife, who not only reared nine sons and four daughters, but was also a charming and competent hostess to innumerable visitors and catered for scores of casual grape-pickers at vintage time. In other ways too, she showed a rare gift for organization.

Oscar, the eldest of Benno's sons, was chairman of directors for twenty-three years. A great figure in the wine industry generally. During the economic depression of the 1930s, he instigated the planting of the palm trees which now grace the approaches to Seppeltsfield and the family mausoleum. Leo followed Oscar as chairman for three years, and was succeeded by Waldemar. Waldemar's son, Ian, is now chairman of the company, and he has made important contributions to the wine industry in general. He is chairman of the Australian Wine Board, President of the Chamber of Manufacturers of South Australia, a member of the Commonwealth Export Development Council, and has travelled widely on export missions. Robert is general manager, and a past president of the Federal Wine and Brandy Producers' Council of Australia and the Wine

## SEPPELT'S AND SEPPELTSFIELD

and Brandy Producers' Association of South Australia. He and John, the sales director, are Leo's sons. Their cousins, Bill and Karl, are concerned with production and vineyards respectively. Bill works in conjunction with Ross Jenkins, the production manager. The fifth generation is now strongly represented by Robert's son, Nicholas, Ian's sons, Malcolm and Graham, and Bill's son, Bill. Nicholas is a graduate of the University of California and manager of Seppeltsfield. Although many of the Seppelt family hold important positions, outside capital has been taken in and the organization will soon be a public company.

A difficulty arises in writing of the Barossa wines of Seppelt's. Many of the wines come in whole or in part from the Valley, but they are frequently blended for uniformity and consistency of style with wines from the other wineries at Great Western and Rutherglen. The sherries—dry, medium and sweet—are Barossa wines, as are the ports. From time to time, special bin wines from the Valley are offered and these represent real Barossa quality. Not all Seppelt's wines come from the Barossa, but the amount of goodwill, generated by Seppelt's for the Valley is enormous. Both the Valley and the wine industry are enriched by Seppeltsfield and Château Tanunda. The little vineyard begun by Joseph Seppelt has come a long way.

# 3
# Gramp's Orlando

IN the Barossa Valley and indeed in the Australian wine industry, G. Gramp & Sons Pty Ltd stand out for their sheer technical competence and thoroughness. Practically every new technical development in winemaking has been adopted in the Orlando cellars, and in many cases, Gramp's has been the first Australian winery to pioneer new equipment and procedures. This has led to the introduction of many new wines, such as Barossa Riesling, Barossa Pearl, Star Wine and others. Wines which have made the name of Orlando a byword for quality and innovation.

The winery has a rather functional appearance and new extensions are always a part of the scene. There is one real delight—the elegant little tasting room deep within the main building, the oldest part of the winery. The old-world atmosphere of this tasting room is in sharp contrast to the sparkling efficiency of the new bottling line in the latest new building, which runs parallel to the main road just north of the winery. This is technology at its expensive best, and perhaps the contrast shows that the proof of technological perfection of wine still lies in the tasting.

Orlando has a long history. It begins with Johann Gramp, born in 1819 at Eichig, close to Kulmbach, in Bavaria. He came to South Australia in 1847 and established himself at Jacob's Creek, a mile north-west of the present Orlando winery. He planted there a small vineyard and made his first wine in 1850 when his son Gustav was born. In 1877, Gustav moved the winery to its present site, and by 1921 he

Vineyards at Rowland Flat—summer

... and vines adorn the floor of the Valley—autumn

The art of the cooper

had built up a successful business with the aid of his sons Hugo and Fred. In 1920 Hugo became managing director. When he was tragically killed in the 'Kyeema' air disaster in 1938, his brother Fred took control. In a recent change-over Fred, eighty-three, retired as chairman. Hugo's son, Colin, has for a number of years been chief executive, and has given dynamic leadership. He is without doubt an achiever, especially in the attainment of new technological targets. Fred's two sons, Sid in Adelaide and Keith in Melbourne, have long been active in management, Sid concentrating on marketing.

The 'Kyeema' disaster was a major tragedy for the wine industry. The 'Kyeema' aircraft crashed at Mount Dandenong near Melbourne on a flight from Adelaide on 25 October, 1938, and Hugo Gramp, Tom Hardy and Sid Hill-Smith all perished. They were travelling together to attend Wine Week and meetings of the Federal Viticultural Council in Melbourne. Charles Hawker, one of the Ministers of the Federal Government, also lost his life in this disaster.

It could be said that Gramp's has had a greater impact on the Australian wine scene than any other winery, by virtue of the introduction of Orlando Barossa Riesling, Barossa Pearl and subsequently, the related wines Pink Barossa Pearl and Sparkling Star Wine. Barossa Pearl was introduced in November 1956, at a time when the Australian wine public was looking particularly for a suitable sparkling wine which had the appeal of champagne, without its high price. Barossa Pearl was the find of the decade and brought with it something of deeper significance. Many Australians who did not previously drink wine were won over by the pleasant bubbly sweet fruitiness of Barossa Pearl, without the associated sulphur dioxide, frequently characteristic of sweet table wines. Barossa Pearl was an expensive wine to produce, because it required large pressure tanks for the secondary fermentation to take place and give sparkle to the wine. The wine had then to be clarified and bottled under pressure of carbon dioxide and this required sophisticated sterile bottling equipment. But the big demand for Barossa Pearl enabled large-scale production and an economical price.

It is important to clarify a misconception about these sparkling pearl-type wines. Some people equate them with carbonated aerated waters, in which the carbon dioxide causing the bubbles is introduced artificially from a cylinder of the gas bought for the purpose. This is not so in winemaking for several reasons. If a wine is carbonated, this must be declared on the label by law. Secondly, carbonated wines (and aerated waters) usually do not keep their sparkle long after opening. The gas bubbles are big and the drink quickly goes flat. Thirdly, in the normal process of fermentation, an enormous amount of carbon dioxide is evolved and this can be put to use. Depending on the sugar content of the grape juice, the quantity of carbon dioxide given off is about forty times the volume of juice fermented. So it can be seen that the winemaker is not short of carbon dioxide. Indeed, dispersal of the gas in the winery sometimes constitutes a problem in confined spaces. If the winemaker can saturate the wine with carbon dioxide by a fermentation with added grape juice or sugar in a large container, he obtains a wine which will hold its sparkle in the same way as champagne, which is refermented in the bottle.

In 1953, Orlando introduced its first Barossa Riesling, made by the German 'controlled fermentation' technique. It was an immediate winner. Hitherto, the Rieslings in Australia had been rather full wines, with a golden colour resulting from wood age and low sulphur dioxide. The controlled fermentation Rieslings were fresher, with a greenish-yellow colour and a pronounced Riesling character. They were bottled young, and could be drunk in the year of making, although they improved even further with bottle aging. Even the oldest wines made in this way have a freshness and character which is quite remarkable.

Gramp's created a trend in these wines, and I well

remember what happened when they were first exhibited in wine shows. This was in the days when the awards were first, second and third prizes, before the gold, silver and bronze medals were introduced. The Orlando Rieslings were consistent prize winners, and it was frequently a case of awarding other wines the minor placings. Gramp's still win awards with Barossa Riesling, but now the competition is keener. Other winemakers are using similar techniques and the general standard of quality in premium dry white wines has been greatly improved.

As we can see, winemaking in the sixties has undergone revolutionary changes with the advent of new equipment to make table wines better and cheaper. Much of this new equipment has been pioneered in Australia by Orlando. The widespread use of centrifuges, the Mac (South African) four-stage press and the pressurator (which drains and presses white grapes under carbon dioxide), the gravity separators and other equipment produces wines of a quality and style previously unattainable.

The use of new types of equipment and procedures based on German practices has resulted in new wine types. Gramp's was the first to produce 'Auslese' and 'Spätlese' wines from selected Riesling and Frontignac grapes. (*Spätlese*, wine made from late-gathered grapes; *Auslese*, wine made from the choicest grape bunches). These names are now also used by other winemakers in the Valley.

In Germany, as well as in certain other parts of Europe, the grapes are sometimes attacked by the fungus *Botrytis cinerea* with, surprisingly, beneficial results. In Australia, *Botrytis* infection of grapes causes rot, but in the cooler, more moist European climate the *Botrytis* infection is sometimes encouraged. The name of the infection is an indication of the importance attached to it—'*Edelfäule*' (noble rot—'*pourriture noble*' in French). The effect of this noble rot is to crack the skin of the berry and allow partial dessication or drying, thereby increasing the sweetness of the juice. The fungus also alters the composition of the juice in other ways, by increasing the content of glycerine, for example. The net effect is that the grape juice is richer in sugar, and has an altered and particularly desirable flavour. The berries do not taste mouldy, but have rather a sweet honey-like flavour.

The high quality German wines are almost all sweet, and many of them result from grapes infected with '*Edelfäule*.' The distinctive names used by Orlando and a few other wineries, so far, are '*Auslese*' and '*Spätlese*'. The former is of higher quality than the latter. In Germany, '*Beeren auslese*' (selected berries or twigs) and '*Trockenbeeren auslese*' (selected dried berries) are also made. Such wines are rare because they depend on propitious climate—not very common in Germany. They are also very sweet because of the low yield of juice. So far these wines have not been made in Australia, for climatic reasons, but we live in hope. Perhaps artificial inoculation of the grapes with *Botrytis* under a controlled environment may be the answer, as has been tried in California. Who knows—perhaps Gramp's may be the people who solve this intriguing and pleasant problem.

Orlando is a winery which tends to make all its wines well, and since the range of wines marketed is now nearly sixty, this is saying something. A good reason for high quality is not only good grapes and equipment but also good technical people. Colin Gramp has gathered an expert team. Günter Prass, the associate technical director and cellar manager, came from Germany with an excellent wine background and extensive experience at the Seitz factory at Bad Kreuznach, which makes equipment for the wine and beverage industries. Mark Tummel is in charge of table wines and Harold Pfeiffer controls the dessert wines. Jeff Virgo operates their impressive laboratory and Tony Kluczko supervises the quality control programme.

Besides the premium Rieslings and Cabernets, Orlando produces Miamba Riesling Hock (a blend of Riesling, Sémillon and Tokay), Miamba Claret, a Moselle and a

White Burgundy, within the middle price range. The Barossa Cabernet (a blend of Cabernet Sauvignon and Shiraz) has achieved wide recognition. Some of the earlier wines tended to be jammy, due probably to overripe grapes, but the recent Cabernets, lighter in style, are fine examples. The wines are given a gentle maturation in French oak, but do not have the pronounced wood character which marks some of our other dry red wines. Gramp's produce some excellent dessert wines and their tawny port is particularly good. They call it 'Vintage Tawny' which is a curious misnomer, since tawny port is almost always a blend of wine from different years to maintain consistency of style.

But times and circumstances change, and the announcement in December 1970 of the takeover of G. Gramp & Sons Pty Ltd by Reckitt & Colman Australia Ltd (a big U.K.-based concern) came as a surprise and a shock to many people. It is sad to see a great and successful winery, with strong historic family associations, lose—or even partially lose—this identity, this uninterrupted family control, after 120 years of operation. However, the demands of jet-age progress, commercially and financially, seem to be inexorable. And there is some consolation in a statement by Colin Gramp that the merger, as he prefers to call it, leaves the family members still on the board of directors. Charles Lawson, the secretary, is also a board member.

The change means enhanced prospects for sales development through Reckitt & Colman's Australia-wide and world-wide distribution networks. The enlarged Orlando board, including three Reckitt & Colman men, considers this will have benefits for Barossa Valley people—for independent grapegrowers, for those families involved in winery and company vineyard employment, and so for the prosperity of the Valley generally. Those benefits will stem from the assurance of adequate capital for further expansion at Rowland Flat and maintenance of intake of Barossa grapes. There should also be adequate marketing resources for the output of the vineyards Gramp's have developed in the past decade in the Murray Valley at Ramco near Waikerie, and for the vineyard plantings on newly-acquired property at Eden Valley, south-east of the Barossa proper.

With Colin's keenness on progress and innovation, it is certain that as long as he has his way the unique Steingarten experiment in the hills behind Orlando will be continued. Established in 1962, it is an experiment in growing white wine grapes at high altitude in rock-riddled soil—to prove again that the vine yields its rarest wine under greatest adversity. In the Barossa, the usual vineyard contains between 450 and 600 vines to the acre. (Usually, the vines are planted twelve feet between rows by seven feet in the rows.) Their Steingarten vineyard (garden of stones) is 1600 feet in altitude, with 2760 vines to the acre (four feet by four feet). Each vine is supported by a tall stake as in the Mosel Valley in Germany. The climate in this high region is not very reliable but in a good year the Steingarten Riesling is one of the finest wines of its type in Australia, and certainly one of the rarest.

Orlando stores about four million gallons of wine at Rowland Flat and has just about every type and style on the market. What would Johann Gramp think if he came back today? It is a far cry from his one octave of wine made at Jacob's Creek in 1850.

# 4
# Yalumba

OF all the wineries in the Barossa Valley, the Yalumba cellars of S. Smith & Son Pty Ltd at Angaston probably present to the visitor the grandest impression of solidarity and tradition, with the castle-like façade rising high among the trees. Behind this solid and austere front lies expertise, sophisticated equipment and a range of fine wines. The sherries and ports are famous; Galway Pipe port is a rationed commodity because the demand continually exceeds the supply. The whites are fine and, in recent years from Pewsey Vale, superb . . . But more of this later.

Samuel Smith came from Dorsetshire and must have been quite a man. He was a staunch, strict Christian, and at nineteen years of age, he was manager of a brewery. Sixteen years later, in 1847, with a wife and five children he set sail for Australia. He arrived in South Australia and moved by bullock wagon to Angaston, where he was appointed to take charge of George Fife Angas's garden. In 1849, he bought thirty acres of the beautiful land around Angaston and called it 'Yalumba', a native word meaning 'all the country around'. There he planted his vineyard.

At about this time, the gold rush was on in Bendigo, Victoria, and Samuel joined it to obtain money to consolidate his property. After four months he returned with £300 which he invested in more land, a homestead and farming equipment. Within ten years the venture was on its feet, and, with his son Sidney, in 1863 he made sixty hogsheads of wine.

Sidney Smith took over on the death of his father in 1888, and was succeeded in turn by his sons Percival and Walter. The latter became a big game hunter, and adorned the Yalumba homestead with trophies from India and Africa. His son, Sid Hill-Smith, later took control of the business, and served until he was killed in the 'Kyeema' air disaster in 1938. Sid's brother Wyndham, who was the Yalumba manager in Perth at the time, returned to Yalumba to become managing director, which office he holds today—the fourth generation. Wyndham is an extraordinarily versatile man. He combines his love of wine and art with a passion for cricket and horses, and he has bred a string of race horses which bear wine names: Cellarmaster, Cellarman, Winemaker, Toastmaster, Galway Pipe and others. Sid's sons, Mark and John, are the fifth generation, and Wyndham's son is now in the winery too.

Two other people, who have long been associated with Yalumba, are particularly well known. Alf Wark is the company secretary, but he is more widely known for his culinary ability, which has earned him an enviable reputation. His recent book *Wine Cookery* is a little gem. Rudi Kronberger is a graduate of the famous Austrian wine school at Klosterneuberg, near Vienna. He brought with him to Australia professional expertise and a knowledge of European wines which have revealed themselves in the quality of the Yalumba wines. Together with Ray Ward, who makes the vintage at the Vintners Co. Pty Ltd (a subsidiary of Yalumba) a few miles away, and Peter Wall who controls bottling and packaging, they make a formidable team.

In discussing Yalumba wines, a moot point arises. Yalumba, like several other large Barossa wineries, has established a vineyard in the Murray Irrigation Area (as well as having vineyards in the Barossa), bringing the grapes to Angaston for winemaking. Are these wines then Barossa wines? For the purpose of this book they are not, and I shall limit a discussion of the wines to those derived wholly or largely from Barossa grapes.

The original cellar at Seppeltsfield, 1851

Seppeltsfield 1876

Yalumba makes no fewer than ten ports. They range in quality from Show port and Galway Pipe, with an average age of fifteen years, to Royal Reserve and V.O. Invalid port, the least expensive and youngest of the range. The name 'Galway Pipe' is interesting. Galway was a former Governor of South Australia who seemed to enjoy visiting Yalumba, and pipes are wooden casks used in Portugal to store port . . . Galway Pipe is made from Shiraz, Dolcetto (a littlegrown black grape) and Tokay (a white grape). The Tokay lightens the colour to a light tawny. The wine is fortified with brandy spirit during making to increase the flavour. This is expensive, because brandy spirit contains less alcohol than fortifying spirit, and more of those other desirable compounds (higher alcohols and esters) which make brandy what it is.

The other ports: Director's Special, Four Crown, V.O. and the others form a gradation in quality and price, being progressively younger and having more Grenache in their makeup. Director's Special, for example, is about ten years old, and Four Crown about seven. V.O. Invalid port in the minimum price group is two years old. With port one pays for age.

There is also a formidable range of sherries—no fewer than ten of them. Most wineries make acceptable sweet sherries, and we shall not concern ourselves with those, except to say that Yalumba amontillado and oloroso are prize wines. Fino sherries, however, are another thing—flor sherries are very hard to make well and take much time and care, because the flor process is technically difficult and needs understanding. Yalumba's top fino sherries— Championship Show Fino, Chiquita and Galway Fino— are all made by a modified Spanish flor process, in which the wine from Palomino, Pedro and some Temperano grapes is placed on flor for several years in oak casks, then aged further after blending and fortifying. Galway Fino is sweetened somewhat to cater for the more popular demand, but the very finest flor sherries from a quality point of view are quite dry. Flor sherries are the driest wines in the world in their unsweetened state, because the flor yeast utilizes the last traces of fermentable sugar.

The white table wines of Yalumba are held in high esteem, especially Carte D'or, which Max Lake in *Classic Wines of Australia* (Jacaranda Press, 1966) listed as the most classical of the Barossa Rieslings. The real impact of Yalumba in recent years has been their new development in white wines—the new series from Pewsey Vale in the Barossa Hills. The first vineyard (one acre) was planted in Pewsey Vale in 1847 by Mr Gilbert. It was abandoned in 1927, but was known to produce fine table wines.

Yalumba established their 150 acre vineyard at Pewsey Vale in 1961 in partnership with Geoffrey Angas Parsons, owner of Pewsey Vale Station. Norman Hanckel, who was on the Yalumba staff at the time, carried out much of the work. The contoured vineyards of Riesling and Cabernet Sauvignon are a delight to the eye and incidentally are the highest vineyards in Australia at 1800 feet. The first of the new Pewsey Vale wines was produced in 1966. In 1970 Yalumba had the joy of seeing their 1969 Pewsey Vale Riesling awarded the Championship at the Royal Sydney Show. I have been judging these wines at various Royal Shows for many years and there is no doubt that the Pewsey Vale Rhine Riesling has become one of the really great Australian Rieslings. The Golden Ridge late-harvested white wine is also noteworthy. It carries some sweetness, which softens the acidity.

The Yalumba dry reds are basically Barossa wines made mainly from Shiraz and Grenache, and blended with selected reds from other areas, such as Southern Vales and Coonawarra. Some of these wines occasionally carry some volatility, but the finest Yalumba reds are indeed fine wines. These are the 'signature wines' which bear signatures on the label. There is Samuel's Blend, Sidney's Blend and Percy's Blend, named after members of the family, and also Oliver's Blend, named after Oliver Jenkinson, a long-time employee at Yalumba. Then comes the Galway range, followed by Four Crown wines and then the least expensive wines. Yalumba also produces a range of fine Vermouths under licence from Martini and Rossi of Turin, Italy.

# 5
# Penfolds and Port

PENFOLDS Wines Pty Ltd is the largest winemaking company in Australia, and the winery at Nuriootpa is both the largest in the company and the largest in the Barossa Valley. It does not show its size from the road, but the winery covers over seven acres and has a storage capacity of five million gallons. The annual grape crush is nearly 20,000 tons. It is a large winery by anyone's standards.

The Nuriootpa cellar was built by Penfolds in 1912 as a feeder winery to the main South Australian winery at Magill, but it grew in size to become the big brother to Magill. The railway line through the Barossa Valley was also built in 1912, and the route planned was directly from Tanunda to Angaston. However, strong representation from Nuriootpa changed the course of the line so that it passed through Nuriootpa, and incidentally right past Penfolds, in a wide curve to Angaston.

The winery at Nuriootpa concentrated on making dessert wines until quite recently, and has become famous for its ports. There are many great ports, for these are wines which Australian winemakers make very well. One of the finest is Penfold's Grandfather port. It has a long history. The 1915 port which started the line was judged excellent and marked for prolonged aging, and some of it, a minute but calculable amount, is still present in current blends of Grandfather port.

Grandfather port is quite sweet by Australian standards.

It is normally eight to nine degrees baumé and high in alcoholic strength (38° to 39° proof spirit) due to preferential evaporation of water during the long period of ageing in oak hogsheads, sixty-five to seventy gallons in capacity. This increase in alcoholic content is significant. In the warm dry climate of the Barossa, the wine gradually evaporates through the porous staves of the cask, and its volume decreases. Due to surface tension effects, water is lost more rapidly than the alcohol, and the wine remaining in the cask becomes richer in alcohol as ageing progresses. When you consider that about three per cent of the wine is lost by evaporation each year, it can be seen that prolonged ageing in wood is an expensive business.

Shiraz is the basic grape variety for Grandfather port, and it is picked very sweet to conserve the sugar. The grapes are frequently up to fifteen or sixteen degrees baumé. Grandfather port is rationed, and both difficult and expensive to obtain, but it is worth the price. The wine is of indefinite age, because of the blending which occurs to maintain continuity of style, but the average age would be at least fifteen years. It is usually sold to hotels where it is retailed by the glass.

Club port is Penfold's top commercial port, and is based on Grandfather port, with some lighter ports made from Mataro and Grenache blended in to lighten the style and reduce the sweetness to between six to seven degrees baumé. The average age is about ten years.

Other ports are made at Nuriootpa including Royal Reserve, the original Australian Royal Reserve port. These wines are aged in oak hogsheads in what is known as the 'Bird Cage', an enormous building with open sides made of wire mesh. The Bird Cage holds one million gallons of port. It is difficult to visualize one million of anything; for example, one million minutes is nearly six years! One million gallons of port requires about 14,000 hogsheads. At $50 each, the mind boggles. There are many factors involved in making large quantities of old port: good grapes, skilful winemaking and blending, care, money—and a lot of patience!

As well as ports, the Kalimna dry reds should be mentioned. The Kalimna winery and its five hundred acres of vineyards, a few miles north of Nuriootpa, were formerly owned by D. & J. Fowler Ltd, wholesale grocers, who made 'Australian Burgundy' for export to Burgoynes in England. Penfold's bought Kalimna in 1944 and developed the vineyards for production of premium grade dry red, which they sell in bottles bearing individual bin numbers and a description of the wine. The Kalimna winery is now a storage cellar with a large hand-carved tunnel in the rock where flor sherry is still matured.

Apart from the port, some dry red and Eden Valley Riesling (Bins 231 and 421) which are fermented at Magill, the other wines made at Nuriootpa lose their Barossa Valley identity when blended and sold under national, rather than regional labels. This winery also makes all the brandy for the Penfold organization, as well as some of the grape spirit used in making the ports and other dessert wines.

Most wineries have their old identities. At Penfold's it was P. A. Scholz, who began as a cellar hand in 1913 and retired 51 years later as manager. His place was taken by a younger man who had already achieved renown in the wine industry—Ray Beckwith. Ray joined Penfold's in 1935, after graduating from Roseworthy College and spending two valuable years at Tintara with Roger Warren and Colin Haselgrove. He became chief chemist for the company in 1951, and his creation of a central control laboratory was a milestone in the industry. Today Michael Ramsay, a graduate from the University of Adelaide, is in charge of the laboratory and Tim Jolly has returned from England via California to become research officer for the company. Tim has a Master's degree from Cambridge and his work takes him to all the cellars in the Penfold organization. Norm Schutz is another old identity in the cellar. He started work in 1934. Les and Kevin Schroeter both occupy important positions in the winery and they began in 1944 and 1948 respectively.

The winery has recently expanded in an area due north towards Tolley, Scott & Tolley Ltd. A new grape receiving station and modern draining and pressing equipment have been installed. Ray Beckwith is proud of the fact that all the installation, with the exception of the South-African designed press and drainers, was carried out by local people. Even the weighbridge was made locally.

# 6
# Saltram of Angaston

THE Adelaide Bacchus Club has a happy custom of donating a bronze plaque to each winery in South Australia when it reaches its one hundredth year of operation. Many wineries bear these plaques and are thus, in this sense, historical landmarks in South Australia. Saltram has been recognized in this way, and has therefore 'come of age' in the historical sense.

William Salter was born in Exeter, England, in 1804 and arrived with his wife and family in South Australia in 1839, only three years after the State was founded. He purchased land in the Barossa Valley, where he settled and built his home 'Mamre Brook', which is still in good condition and forms part of the present homestead. He raised cattle and sheep and even successfully mined copper on his property. When the price of copper fell in the sixties, he closed the mine.

William Salter & Son was founded in 1859 by William Salter and his son Edward, and vines were planted in that year. The first wine was made in 1862. It must have been fun as well as hard work. All the grapes (Shiraz) were crushed by treading, and this practice continued up to 1891 when steam power was introduced. At this time the maturing and marketing of Saltram wines were being handled by Thomas Hardy & Son of Adelaide. Saltram must have made some fine wines even in those early days, since they were awarded many medals in overseas exhibitions. Leslie

Storage vat at Yalumba

Salter took over management in 1910, and became distinguished in industry and public affairs, including twenty years' membership of the Australian Wine Board as an original member, and three years as chairman.

Saltram became associated with Stonyfell Vineyards (H. M. Martin & Son Pty Ltd) in 1920, and in 1941 became a wholly-owned subsidiary. Today the Saltram winery works in close co-operation with the Stonyfell winery at Burnside. The winemaking is now carried out at Saltram, and Stonyfell is used for maturing and bottling.

Many of the Barossa wineries have employees who have given very long service. Few, if any, could equal the late Fred Ludlow who spent sixty-three years in the Saltram vineyard and winery. He claimed to be the first to introduce sweet sherry (made from Albillo) and actually blended it in a solera system.

Bryon Dolan was the manager of Saltram until he was transferred in 1959 to Stonyfell vineyards at Burnside to become general manager of H. M. Martin & Son Pty Ltd, which owns both Stonyfell and Saltram. His place at Saltram was taken by Peter Lehmann, born at Angaston in 1930, the son of a Lutheran pastor. Peter first worked at Yalumba which he joined in 1947, and developed a knowledge and love of both table and dessert wines under Rudi Kronberger. Saltram has concentrated largely on high quality table wines and port, and developed a brisk trade in supplying quality table wines in bulk for home bottling.

The Saltram vineyards comprise two hundred acres at present, largely planted with high quality varieties such as Cabernet Sauvignon, Shiraz, Rhine Riesling and Clare Riesling. These vineyards receive a useful five inches of supplementary irrigation during the growing season, and supply about ten per cent of the total grape intake, the balance being supplied from other vineyards in the Barossa, as well as from Langhorne Creek and other areas.

Following the cessation of winemaking at Stonyfell, the Saltram winery has been modernized and enlarged to a million gallons capacity. This development has deeply involved Peter Lehmann, Bryon Dolan and Henry Martin, the managing director. The result is a well-equipped functional winery with some of the latest in new equipment, and the wines reflect both the modern procedures and the skill of the winemaker.

Peter Lehmann has adopted the practice of lightening the style of some of the Saltram dry reds (they were formerly big, dark, astringent wines which aged slowly) by blending in a small quantity of Tokay to produce the softer full-flavoured burgundy style now identified with Saltram. The Saltram clarets show the benefit of more and more Cabernet Sauvignon as these grapes become available from the new plantings, and two distinct styles of dry red are made —the soft full-flavoured burgundy and the more austere astringent claret.

Traditionally, Saltram has been known for dry red and sweet sherry, but much more is now available. The Alameda tawny port made from Shiraz, Tokay and Semillon receives wide acclaim, as does the occasional vintage port from Shiraz and Cabernet Sauvignon, fortified with brandy spirit. Peter Lehmann's experience at Yalumba has helped him greatly with his range of sherries, and he is also an oenological humorist at heart—his Zugspitze Birnenwein comes as a surprise, made from Duchess pears grown near Angaston. He also makes an apple wine.

The wines to look for particularly are the selected vintage table wines, at present the Bin 51 Claret and Bin 49 Burgundy, the soft full-flavoured White Burgundy made from Semillon, Clare Riesling and Tokay, and Rhine Riesling made by controlled cold fermentation with the new refrigeration plant. The 1958 vintage port is a fine example of a late-bottled vintage port, and comes in part from the Barossa and in part from Langhorne Creek.

# 7
# Henschke and the Hill of Grace

ABOUT eight miles south-east of Angaston, near the village of Keyneton, stands a small Lutheran church close to a vineyard. The church is called 'Gnadenberg' (Hill of Grace) and gives its name to the vineyard and to the red wine from the vineyard. In an area where rich and euphonious names abound, 'Hill of Grace' could well be unique as a name for a vineyard and its wine. In the Lutheran tradition of the Valley it is singularly appropriate.

Hill of Grace is one of three red wines made by C. A. Henschke & Co.; the other two are Mount Edelstone and Hermitage. Mount Edelstone is an anglicized version of Mount Edelstein (noble stone) and the wine from this vineyard has been a consistent prizewinner since 1952. In addition to the three red wines, Henschke markets a range of whites as varietal wines; Riesling, Frontignac, Semillon, Ugni Blanc and Sercial. Sercial is a white grape which is, in South Australia, almost wholly confined to the Barossa.

One important feature of Henschke wines is that they are all entirely regional. All the grapes come from the area and Cyril Henschke has recently established a new vineyard of seventy acres in a frost-free area about two miles north of Eden Valley, on the main road between Eden Valley and Angaston. The main grape varieties are those known to make top quality Barossa wines—Riesling and Shiraz.

Johann Christian Henschke was born in Jutschlau, Silesia, in 1803. He emigrated to Australia in 1842 with

213 migrants in the ship *Skjold* taking ninety-eight days. He settled in Bethany, a few miles south-east of Tanunda. A builder and mason, he built the original winery at Keyneton, where he made his first wine in 1868. Wine has been made continuously at Henschke's by Johann's son Paul (1847-1914), by his son Paul Alfred (1878-1964), and then by Cyril, born in 1924. Cyril's elder son, Paul again, born in 1949, recently completed a science degree at the Adelaide University. His younger son Stephen is still at the University and plans to come home to Keyneton when he graduates. Cyril, accompanied by his wife Doris, recently spent some months in Germany on a Churchill Fellowship, the first awarded in Australia to a winemaker.

In the wine industry one does not have to be big to make good wine. It helps, but size has not any direct relationship to quality. Henschke wines have won many awards and are well known among wine lovers, and this is probably because Cyril Henschke makes the wines he knows. The winery is only part of the Henschke property. Cyril owns about 700 acres, but has only 140 of these planted with vines. He crushed only about 400 tons of grapes during vintage. The winery has certain features; it is small, not highly mechanized or even modern, and it makes only table wines. Cyril Henschke is doing what many other men and some women would love to do—making the natural wines of the district.

Keyneton is in a sense apart from the Barossa Valley. It is near to it, but not of it. The area is marginal viticulturally. The average rainfall is 21.5 inches, but it fluctuates widely from year to year. The soils are different from those in the Valley, the land is higher and it has the occasional winter frost. Thus the wines have a different character. The winery is relatively remote from others in the Valley and has an atmosphere of age and solidarity.

The Henschke winery holds a cherished position in the Valley. It is a family operation now in the fifth generation of continuous ownership. The centenary of the winery was celebrated in 1968 with a simple, dignified and touching ceremony, and its entry into its second century augurs well for the future.

# 8
# Kaiser Stuhl

OF all the wineries in the Valley, probably none has shown such rapid growth as Kaiser Stuhl, the Barossa Co-operative Winery Ltd of Nuriootpa. It is one of seven co-operative wineries in South Australia and the only such co-operative in the Valley. With a work force of over 250, its expansion is a tribute to the management. Oscar Semmler from Lyndoch is chairman and chief executive officer, George Kolarovich is the technical director and winery manager and Robert Litchfield is secretary. Oscar Semmler's grandparents settled in Hofnungstal near Lyndoch over a hundred years ago.

The Barossa Co-operative Winery is not particularly old as wineries go. Grapegrowers in the Valley banded together at the height of the Depression in May 1931, forming a co-operative to process surplus grapes. The early years were difficult and markets were scarce. The main outlet in the pre-war period was through export to the United Kingdom. But in the last twenty years, progress has been rapid as the co-operative marketed more and more of its wines under its own label. In 1958, the Kaiser Stuhl name first appeared on the label and this heralded the introduction of many fine wines, to the delight and financial benefit of the 450 grower-shareholders.

Kaiser Stuhl (the Seat of Kings) was the name given to the flat-topped hill on the eastern side of the Barossa Valley, overlooking the vineyards on the floor and slopes of the Valley. It reminded the pioneering German settlers of a hill of the same name close to the Rhine, a few miles north of Freiburg in southern Germany. Perhaps we should not carry the analogy too far . . . Many of the pioneering German settlers came from Silesia, four hundred miles northeast of Kaiser Stuhl in southern Poland, and Kaiser Stuhl is an isolated mountain (1730 feet high) rising from the plain of the Rhine Valley, whilst its namesake is part of the Barossa Hills, which are in turn part of the Mount Lofty Ranges . . . However, it is a romantic name and properly belongs in the Barossa Valley. It is interesting to to recall that Kaiser Stuhl was renamed Mt Kitchener during the extraordinary period of indignant patriotic fervour that occurred at the time of the First World War. Fortunately, the Germanic name ultimately prevailed.

The trend for Germanic names is catching. Not far south on the Sturt Highway from Kaiser Stuhl (the winery, not the hill), at the Dorrien corner, is *'Die Weinstube'*, a restaurant set in a vineyard and run by John Davenport and Dennis Hahn. You may fill your car with petrol at *'Die Barossa Tankstelle'* at Lyndoch if you wish!

One can talk with eloquence on the Kaiser Stuhl wines. The clarets, Rieslings, rosé and sparkling wines are particularly well known. As with most large wineries, the entire range of wines is offered—the number on a recent listing was fifty, including vermouth, marsala all'uovo and six types of sherry! The rosé introduced late in 1962 was a winner and a trend-setter in the industry, particularly when it was presented in a distinctive new bottle in 1967.

In Australia it is difficult, and frequently impossible, to buy a wine and know *exactly* where it comes from. This is a reasonable and perennial grouch for many winelovers, and one feels a good deal of sympathy for this view. In fact, some wines are as anonymous as tomato sauce. Kaiser Stuhl was the first winery to produce individual vineyard wines, made from grapes grown in a particular vineyard, owned by a particular person who was named on the label.

This was a wonderful idea. You knew precisely where the wine came from, and the wines were also very well made. The first Individual Vineyard wines were made in 1958, in Ian Hickinbotham's time, from Riesling grapes grown in Eric Stephens' vineyard 'Wyncroft' in Eden Valley. George Kolarovich continued and expanded the idea, and now W. C. & R. V. Rogers' Riesling of Eden Valley is featured. If the wine is a dry Riesling the bottle carries a green neck ribbon, whilst a gold ribbon signifies a sweet late-harvest wine. The label also carries a classification table which is meant to indicate to the buyer the company's opinion of the wine. The lowest score so far is five points out of a possible ten, and some wines have rated the maximum ten points. At the end of 1970, the first Individual Vineyard red wine was presented. This was a 1966 Shiraz dry red made from grapes grown on A. E. Materne's property at Greenock. The bottle carries a red neck ribbon. These Individual Vineyard wines are today distinctive as Kaiser Stuhl premium wines.

Most wineries in Australia exhibit wines in wine shows conducted by the Royal Agricultural Societies in Sydney, Melbourne, Adelaide, Brisbane and Perth, and these shows have done much to raise the overall quality of Australian wines. Kaiser Stuhl wines have won numerous awards, in which makers and shareholders take much pride. They are particularly pleased to win awards in overseas wine exhibitions, such as the one at Montpellier in France. The large cellar below the winery contains hundreds of hogsheads of imported French oak, tronçais and nevers, holding clarets in cool maturation. Care is needed to win awards.

Kaiser Stuhl's greatest contribution is probably in the low cost sparkling wine field, in which they have followed Gramp's lead. They have made millions of bottles, not only for the Kaiser Stuhl label, but also for various other companies. The impact of this type of wine on Australians, particularly young Australians, has been very great. Not only does it give young folk a taste for wine, without the

Benno Seppelt

Samuel Smith—
the founder of Yalumba

An early photograph taken at Seppeltsfield of horse-drawn carts arriving with loads of grapes

The new grape-processing and pressing cellar at Orlando stands on the site where this large red gum was felled

over-abundance of sulphur dioxide in some of our sauternes of former years, but it also leads them into the finer vinous experience of the table wines.

High quality and sophisticated equipment are necessary for making these wines, and the day of the technologist is here. Some parts of Kaiser Stuhl are as far removed from a traditional winery as one can get. Such items as automatic horizontal presses, self-emptying centrifuges, thermostatically controlled pressure tanks, and fully automatic bottling lines represent big money and big responsibility. They also enable the winemaker to make these sparkling wines in the proper way.

The people who operate this equipment are well trained. George Kolarovich came from Yugoslavia and is an Agricultural Science graduate from Munich University. He joined the company in 1961. Neville Wilson, Bob Cartwright and Brian Falkenberg hold Diplomas of Oenology from Roseworthy Agricultural College. Jim Smyth holds a Diploma of Chemistry from the University of Adelaide, and Hubert Faseth has a Diploma of Oenology and Viticulture from the famous wine school at Klosterneuberg near Vienna. Bryce Hood is also involved in quality control, a very important aspect of winemaking, since expansion is a continual part of the scene at Kaiser Stuhl. At present a new modern bottling hall is being built to accommodate the latest bottling and bottle packaging equipment, with an output of 8000 bottles per hour.

You will notice that the word 'make' is used instead of 'manufacture' when speaking of wines. One manufactures a motor car, one builds a house, but one makes wine. Sometimes a winery like Kaiser Stuhl somewhat resembles a chemical engineering plant, when viewed from a certain angle, and the distinction between make and manufacture becomes blurred, but the concept remains. One builds on nature—the miracle of fermentation—and wine is made, not manufactured. The term 'fabricate' would be quite out of place.

One final word—we all have our likes and dislikes. I like the grape receiving and crushing department of a winery to be well-designed, easy to operate and keep clean and, if possible, attractive to the eye. There is an aesthetic angle here. Fine grapes should be handled properly with neat and clean equipment. Kaiser Stuhl has a fine crushing plant. Kaiser Stuhl has come a long way since its formation in the difficult years of the depression. The wines are now sold Australia-wide and set a high standard for quality.

# 9
# Tolley, Scott & Tolley

TOLLEY, Scott & Tolley Ltd at Nuriootpa is an old identity in the Valley, and has established a reputation for quality T.S.T. brandy. The company was taken over in 1961 by the Distillers Company Ltd in England, and has branched out into winemaking as well as continuing its distillation programme. Gordon Nilsson was formerly manager at T.S.T. His place was taken by a young German who had already built a reputation as a maker of fine table wines—Wolfgang Blass. Wolf was originally at Kaiser Stuhl, before setting himself up as a consultant to some of the smaller South Australian winemakers. He was responsible for lifting the quality of their table wines. A number of wine show awards resulted from his efforts, and his new association with Phil Tummel at T.S.T. should result in a flow of quality table wines, particularly from the newly established vineyard in the Eden Valley being organized by John McNeil. Already T.S.T. has won awards for its table wines and the future looks very promising.

The winery at Nuriootpa was acquired in 1895 and it has been greatly expanded and modernized recently to enter the quality table wine field. The grapes come from the Barossa and the new plantings at Eden Valley. In addition, the 1000 acre irrigated vineyard established in 1967 near Waikerie provides grapes for T.S.T. brandy, which enjoys wide sales in Australia. Lance Ackland the managing director, Bob Wade the secretary, Phil Tummel the production manager, and Wolf Blass have much to be proud of in their achievements. Tolley, Scott & Tolley is a company to watch. It is too early yet to list particular wines, but we can expect some very good examples in the future.

# 10
# Château Leonay

THE visitor to the Barossa Valley may easily miss Château Leonay as he drives northward from Tanunda towards Nuriootpa. The winery is built low down on the east bank of the North Para River, and is almost invisible from the road. However, for a winelover to miss Château Leonay would be a serious error, for it houses some of Australia's finest wines, as well as one of Australia's most noted winemakers, John Vickery.

One of the problems in describing wineries in the Valley is that their appearance may change radically with time. A description now may be accurate and meaningful, but in a short time it may be quite inaccurate. It is remarkable how much a row of large stainless steel tanks can alter their appearance. This is what is happening to Château Leonay. The winery looks different on each successive visit, and the large new buildings, the new laboratory, and additional outside stainless steel storage are going to render any present description rather meaningless in the future. Château Leonay is growing at a great rate and Reg Shipster, the manager, and John Vickery have much work on their hands.

After having been associated with other enterprises, Leo Buring formed his own business, Leo Buring Pty Ltd in Sydney in 1931, and made its name by the production and intensive selling of a semi-sweet white table wine, Rinegolde, in a distinctive broadbased green bottle. In the 1930s,

41

Rinegolde was the only wine that many people knew. The name came from the German 'reines gold', meaning 'pure gold', which referred to the wine's colour, and not to any association with Rhine wine. Recently, a pearl-type version of Rinegolde was introduced and has proved to be very popular.

In 1945 Leo Buring purchased a small winery on the North Para river, built by Gottlieb Hoffman in 1907. The winery was rebuilt and expanded with the object of establishing a solidly built, Flemish-style château. The object was very nearly achieved, but Leo Buring's death in 1961 intervened and the château was never wholly completed. Bigger interests took over and the winery expanded at a great rate with the addition of large modern buildings which now house the vintaging equipment, pressure fermentation, bottling and warehousing. The storage is modern and extensive, built to hold vintages which have increased from sixty-five tons in the first year to over 5,000 tons at the present time.

Château Leonay is part of Leo Buring Pty Ltd which is now a wholly-owned subsidiary of Lindeman's Wines Ltd. Thus, Château Leonay can call on the expertise of such people as Ray Kidd, Phillip Laffer and Ron Prince of Lindemann's. There is still a personal link with the late Leo Buring through Reg Shipster, who received his training from Leo Buring.

The vintage cellar at Château Leonay houses some of the most modern equipment, and the white winemaking is a continuous process being handled through special drainers, and a continuous pneumatic press, the third to be installed in South Australia. The final pressing is through a very large thirty-two inch screw press, the biggest of its kind in Australia. Small batch processing of the premium quality grapes is handled through air-bag presses, and the utmost care is taken to produce very high quality white wines. The red wines are fermented in enclosed stainless steel tanks instead of the ubiquitous open concrete fermenters. These tanks are more modern, more convenient to operate, and make fine wines.

Château Leonay produces nearly forty different wines of all types, and their Rieslings are quite outstanding. They certainly rank with the very best in Australia. As with the dry red wines, four separate qualities are offered. The top premium wines appear as Reserve Bins with a white label and special bin numbers, followed by the Private Bins, which have a black background label. These comprise the Riesling (Bin 33), moselle (21), claret (7) and burgundy (13). Then follows the colourful Château Leonay label (which is printed in Germany) and finally, the least expensive wines, curiously called Extra Special. The Reserve Bin wines are chosen from successful show wines, and for the discriminating drinker (preferably on an expense account), both the reds and whites are magnificent wines. For the discriminating drinker *without* an expense account, the Château Leonay range of table wines represents very good value. It is always handy to have a 'best buy'. The reds have desirable characteristics of lightness and delicacy with admirable balance and flavour. The chablis and white burgundy are good styles and show the care and attention given to winemaking, for these are wines which are difficult to make well. The Leo Buring technical team—Reg Shipster, John Vickery, Mostyn Kaesler and Richard Baldwin—know winemaking principles and practice very well.

There are many fine wines in the Leo Buring range, and the two top sherries, Florita dry flor and Oloroso, deserve special mention. They are both prize winners and very commendable wines. Florita is actually the name of a vineyard at Watervale owned by Leo Buring Pty Ltd, which was acquired from Malcolm Allan a few years after Château Leonay was established. Leo Buring wines also include no few than seven sparkling wines and Liebfraumilch.

The success of Château Leonay is best shown in their recent wine show awards. In 1969, 85 awards were obtained from 122 entries and in 1970, 98 awards out of 145 entries.

This is quite remarkable, and some of the wines also won individual trophies as well as gold, silver and bronze awards. It is occasionally said that you (meaning the customer) cannot buy the award-winning wines because they are kept for the directors and are not available to the public. This may be so with a few very special wines with a few companies, but wines are made to be sold, and even directors have a limit to their capacity! Reg Shipster assures me that all the Château Leonay wines exhibited for wine show awards are commercial wines and are available under one or other of the labels. This is as it should be.

St Hallett's Winery at Tanunda

Wilsford Winery at Lyndoch

# 11
# Basedow's Wines

THE location of O. Basedow Wines Ltd is the first surprise to the visitor. It is right on Sturt Highway leading northward from Tanunda and in the middle of a residential district. The second surprise is the quality of the wines. The winery was established before the turn of the century and the present manager, John Basedow, represents the fourth generation of the family to be engaged in winemaking.

All the wines are made from grapes grown in the Valley and the winery has become known for dry reds, whites and ports. Many show awards have been won by these wines, including a gold medal in Adelaide in 1969 and the Jimmy Watson Prize in Melbourne in 1970 for the 1969 Cabernet-Shiraz dry red. The Rieslings have also been prize winners. The wines are essentially regional wines representative of the Barossa Valley. Good things sometimes come in small parcels, and Basedow's wines should not be overlooked because they come from a small winery.

# 12
# Hoffmann's of North Para

ON the west bank of the North Para in Tanunda, just across the river from Château Leonay, lies the winery of Hoffmann's North Para Wines Pty Ltd. Laurel Hoffmann M.B.E. and her late husband, Erwin, were together renowned for their hospitality in the Valley, and contributed a great deal to charity over a long period. The green lawn shaded by stately eucalyptus trees between the river and the winery has been the venue for many happy barbecues and festivities.

The winery is one of the smaller installations in the Valley, and is now controlled by Erwin's and Laurel's son, Bruce, the fifth generation Hoffmann to make wine on this site. Such is the wine industry in the Valley, that a winery such as North Para can trace its history unbroken from 1847, when Samuel Hoffmann arrived in the ship *Gellert* from Silesia with his wife, one daughter and eight sons. Samuel Hoffmann and Johann Gramp were the first to plant vines in the Valley in 1847. There are now over three thousand descendants from this family in Australia, and Bruce's three sons, Stephen, Gregory and Roderick, represent the sixth generation living on the original site.

As with most of the other small wineries in the Valley, the North Para winery has concentrated on dessert wines and dry red, and produces a good range. Wines to look for particularly are some of the old dessert wines, and the 1965 Shiraz-Mataro claret.

# 13
# St Hallett's Wines

As wineries go in the Valley, St Hallett's Wines Pty Ltd is a youngster. It was founded in 1944, but the Lindner family who own it can trace their Australian history back to 1860, when their forbears arrived from Silesia and settled in the Valley at Bethany. Winemaking is a relatively recent development for the family, and the winery in its present form is the work of Carl Wilhelm (Bill) Lindner, who who gained his experience at Gramp's winery at Rowland Flat and later decided to begin winemaking on his own account.

St Hallett's winery is named after Hallett's Valley where the first vines for the winery were planted. The cellar has been enlarged in several stages and has a present capacity of 200,000 gallons. The enlargement has resulted from the demand for table wines and the new underground cellar has a capacity for one million bottles. The winery is a family concern, with Bill and his wife, Norma, and their two sons—Carl, who manages the vineyards, and Elmore, who manages the cellar. The family owns 140 acres of grapes in the Valley, of which fifty acres can be irrigated in dry years from two bores.

St Hallett's offers nearly thirty wines of all types, including sparkling wines. Usually, a winery has certain special wines which it reveres, and in the case of St Hallett's, these are three old dessert wines; a 1959 Pedro Ximenes Oloroso Sherry, a 1954 Port and even a 1944 Port. For their age and price, they are excellent value. The dry reds are distinctive wines and typical of the area. The 1965 Shiraz-Grenache is the oldest dry red wine in the cellar at present, and represents real Barossa Valley quality.

# 14
# Glen View and Matara

THE Glen View winery of P. T. Falkenberg Ltd on the eastern rim of the Valley, near the historic little hamlet of Kabminye, was acquired in 1970 by a newly-formed Melbourne company, Matara Pty Ltd. The managing director is Jim Irvine, a man widely known in the wine industry, who lived as a boy in the Valley. Jim was with Thomas Hardy & Sons Pty Ltd for many years. He worked under the late Roger Warren and Dick Heath at Mile End and with Bob Hagley at McLaren Vale. He was also manager of Siegersdorf and state manager of Hardy's in Victoria.

Matara is in the quality table wine field and has built a new table winemaking installation behind the existing winery. It is too early yet to discuss the wines but we can expect some fine wines from Jim Irvine. The Glen View cellars are situated in a beautiful area, sufficiently high above the valley floor to provide a panoramic view of the Tanunda-Nuriootpa district.

# 15

# Hardy's Siegersdorf

As a name for a winery in the Barossa Valley and for a premium Riesling wine, Siegersdorf is a winner. Hardy's built the winery in 1920 and called it 'Vine Vale' and later 'Dorrien'. Jim Irvine was the manager at Dorrien from 1959 to 1965, after working in the Tintara cellars at Mile End with Dick Heath and the late Roger Warren, who died in March 1960. He proposed the name 'Siegersdorf', which was the original name for the area. In fact, the tiny cemetery near the railway line at Dorrien was originally called Siegersdorf cemetery.

The winery was designed for dessert wines, as were most of the wineries in the Valley, and the change to table wines is quite recent. The first Rhine Riesling dry white wine was made at Dorrien in 1964 from Riesling grapes grown at Eden Valley and Springton, and the name Siegersdorf was first used in 1966. In fact, the winery now makes about ninety per cent table wines, and the Siegersdorf Rhine Riesling has been a great success. The wine is fermented cold without pressure, and clarified, stabilized and bottled quite early, sometimes within three months of making. Thus it retains its youthful freshness and aroma, and conserves the light golden colour of the wine. Dry red wines are also made at Siegersdorf but they are not yet marketed under the Siegersdorf label. Perhaps John Voumard the manager, and John Fanto the winemaker, may start a new fashion in dry red naming.

Tintara also make a fine Eden Moselle from Clare Riesling with a touch of sweetness from Sauvignon Blanc. It is made in the same way as the Riesling with cool fermentation in stainless steel and bottled young.

# 16
# Rovalley Wines

The Rovalley winery of B. Liebich & Sons at Rowland Flat nestles in one of the most attractive parts of the Valley, surrounded by vines and close to the winding North Para River. The winery is adjacent to the Sturt Highway and has expanded considerably in recent years, justifying its transfer from the small to medium-sized group of wineries in the Valley.

Rovalley wines have a surprisingly wide distribution. Much of Rovalley's business is involved with small bulk parcels of wine to hotels. The company owns 650 acres in the Valley of which 400 acres are planted to vines.

Benno Paul Liebich established Rovalley winery in 1918 when he was twenty-eight years of age. When he died in 1941, his two sons C.W. ('Darkie') and H.K. ('Mick') took over its operation. C. W. Liebich is the technical manager and H. K. Liebich is sales manager. Benno had a love of racehorses and both his sons have inherited the same interest.

The winery now has a storage capacity of half a million gallons. A range of nearly twenty wines is offered, many in both bottles and flagons, and almost all wine types are made. The most successful recent wine is the 1970 Rhine Riesling, which won a gold medal in the 1970 Adelaide Wine Show. A recent release in 1969 was Rovalley's sparkling wine 'Charmane' followed in 1970 by a pink version. These wines are made in pressure tanks on the premises. Rovalley also markets a vintage claret made from Shiraz (Hermitage) grown in the Valley.

Fred and Hugo Gramp unloading grapes, 1914

A jewel of the Ba
Château Yaldara at L

Unloading grapes at Orlando, 1927

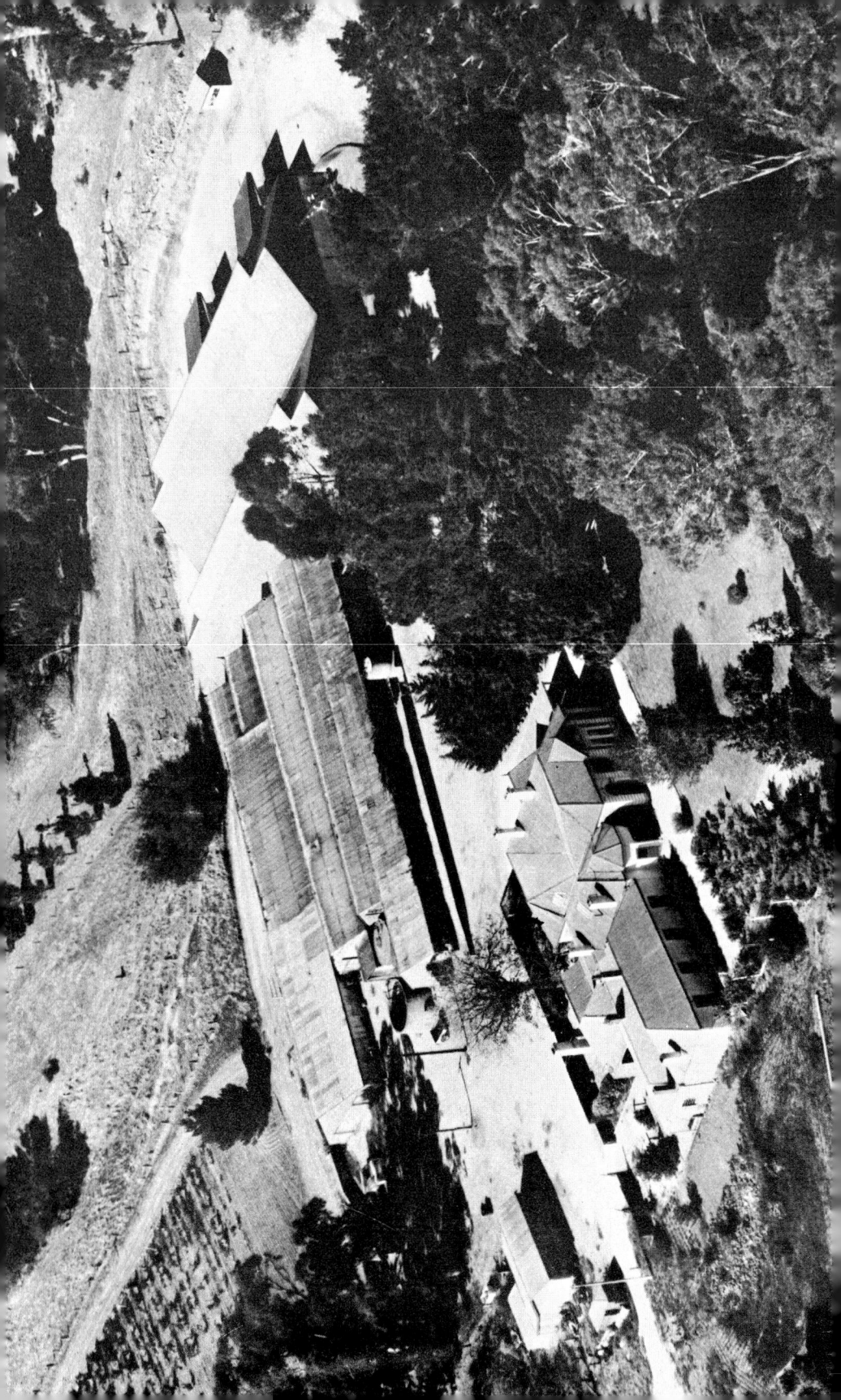

# 17
# Château Yaldara

CHÂTEAU Yaldara Pty Ltd is unique. Winemaking is in many ways an art, and some wineries associate their cellars with minor artistic displays, but Yaldara is superb. The Château has to be seen to be believed. Filled with art treasures, it is modelled along the lines of a formal Château or Schloss in Europe.

Yaldara is one of those wineries which are difficult to describe because change is always evident. The original cellars situated on the bank of the North Para River soon proved to be too small, and a fine new vintage cellar was built on top of the hill overlooking the river and the original cellar. Now a new champagne cellar is under construction due south across an ornamental lake. A short distance further, near the intersection of the Sturt Highway and the Gomersal road at Lyndoch, stands the new Barossa Motel, created by the man who built Yaldara.

Hermann Thumm is one of the new generation German migrants. He arrived in the Valley in 1946, almost one hundred years after his predecessors. He worked in a winery in the Valley for a year, then took over the shell of a former winery. From this he created Château Yaldara, now one of the famous names in the Valley. His elder son, Robert, is at the famous wine college at Geisenheim on the Rhine in Western Germany, and Dieter, his younger son, is studying economics at the University of Adelaide. Both his sons are preparing to take their part in Yaldara, and a new family line is being established in the true tradition of the Valley.

Armin Hebart, a brother-in-law of Hermann Thumm, joined Yaldara in 1960 to become general manager and secretary. Armin is a graduate in science from the University of Adelaide, and taught chemistry and physics at Immanuel College in Adelaide. Both Ewald Walker, head cellarman, and Robert Walter his assistant, came from Germany, and Hermann Deboy, the champagne maker, came from Alsace.

Château Yaldara makes the wide range of wines characteristic of most of the wineries in the Valley, but its special expertise is in the field of sparkling wines. These form a large part of its business. No fewer than thirteen sparkling wines are produced, and their top range, bearing the Great Barossa label, is made by bottle fermentation. Then come the Sekt wines (sekt means 'sparkling wine' in German) which are made by bulk fermentation, and come in a range of sweetness. These wines are keenly priced and enjoy wide popularity. Schiller wine is a speciality—a pink still wine with a touch of sweetness.

Various other sweet wines are made, including a spätlese Riesling and, surprisingly, a sweet claret labelled 'Vintage Claret', which has a curious history. The 1964 vintage was very large and resulted in a glut of grapes. Growers were at their wits' end to know what to do with the grapes, which were becoming riper and riper on the vine. Hermann Thumm decided to process as many of these grapes as he could for the benefit and stability of the industry, even though it meant hasty building of new handling and storage facilities. The result was that some of the claret made from these overripe grapes remained sweet after the fermentation, because the yeast could not ferment all the sugar. He decided on the unprecedented move of marketing a sweet claret, which Armin Hebart named 'Vintage Claret', after the vintage which caused it all. The wine was an immediate success and is now a regular feature.

The aspect of Château Yaldara which immediately

impresses the visitor is the amount of money, time and care which has gone into making the Château and its surroundings an aesthetic and picturesque beauty spot. This is Thumm's deliberate policy and it has everything to commend it. Winemaking is not only an ancient but an honourable institution, and the means by which wine is made and the buildings and grounds associated with it should also be aesthetically attractive. One must pay tribute to Hermann Thumm and his staff.

# 18
# Wilsford Wines

THE Burge family—Percy and his sons Noel and Colin—have operated Wilsford Wines Pty Ltd continuously since 1928, and they make a wide range of appetizer, table and dessert wines. The winery was actually started many years previously by John Burge, Percy's father, who came from England in 1859. Noel was one of the first students to graduate from the oenology course at Roseworthy Agricultural College in 1936. His son Richard and Colin's son Grant represent the fourth generation of the Burge family. Most of the wines are made from grapes grown locally in the pleasant Lyndoch area of the Valley, where yields of between two and four tons per acre are usual. Wilsford Winery was originally designed for dessert wines, and these are still the main types made. However, now the emphasis is turning more to table wines, and new French oak is being used to mature the dry reds.

The winery crushes about 500 tons of grapes, and more than half of these come from the ninety acres owned by the company. The plantings are Rhine Riesling, Cabernet Sauvignon, Shiraz and Clare Riesling. As well as the wide range of dessert wines, the types to look for particularly are the Lyndoch dry reds (especially if they have some bottle age) and the Private Bin port which is a blend of Shiraz and Grenache from 1954, 1959 and 1964.

# 19
# Château Rosevale

CHÂTEAU Rosevale winery is somewhat removed from the Valley. It is near the tiny village of Gomersal, where the land about is devoid of vines, but the Château owns a small vineyard in the Valley. The winery does not look like a Château from the outside, but inside it is a hive of activity.

The place was formerly Fromm's winery, and was taken over in 1964 by Waldemar Lehmann and his son-in-law, Ron Burton, for the purpose of making wines which the public wanted. The range of wines, liqueurs and spirits now available reaches the astounding figure of over one hundred, and all the wines and liqueurs are made on the premises. Château Rosevale specializes in sparkling wines of various kinds, made in pressure tanks. This kind of varied production requires hard work and expertise, and Wally Lehmann and Ron Burton, Dean Kraehenbuhl, the winemaker (formerly with Gramp's and St Hallett's) and Ted Kelly, the engineer, have a busy time.

The winery is quite old, but is rapidly being modernized and will change rapidly in external appearance. Every imaginable type of wine is made, including the curiosity 'Vin-spa', a low alcohol effervescent wine with muscat overtones, which is bottled in crown-sealed bottles. Plans are under way for making and maturing high quality white and red table wines. These will supplement the wide range of other wines which enjoy popular demand.

# 20
# Hamilton's of Springton and Eden Valley

ALTHOUGH Hamilton's Ewell Vineyards Pty Ltd have their headquarters in Marion in the southern suburbs of Adelaide, the company operates two small wineries in Springton and Eden Valley, which produce high quality regional wines.

The Springton winery is the more important of the two and is quite old. It was built by William Rayner in about 1890, on land which originally belonged to Oscar Benno Seppelt. The winery was acquired by Hamilton's in 1938 and largely rebuilt (on the gravity principle) towards the end of the Second World War. The winery has always made table wines, even when the demand was for dessert types, and it is the home of Hamilton's Springton Riesling—one of Australia's fine Rieslings.

The Eden Valley winery was built by Penfold's in 1922, at the beginning of the wine boom which occurred after the First World War. It was acquired by Hamilton's in 1965. A subsidiary company, Eden Valley Wines & Vineyards Pty Ltd, operates the winery and the associated 105 acre vineyard, which is planted with quality table wine varieties such as Shiraz, Cabernet Sauvignon, Riesling, Malbec and White Frontignac. The wines retain their identity and are bottled under the Eden Valley Wines and Vineyards label. Both wineries have refrigeration and stainless steel equipment, and Murray Marchant from the Marion Ewell winery makes the wines.

## HAMILTON'S OF SPRINGTON AND EDEN VALLEY

The wines from both wineries are all quality table wines. The Springton Rhine Riesling and the Hermitage dry red have won many prizes. Claret, burgundy, white Frontignac and occasionally a spätlese Rhine Riesling are made. The moselle is particularly popular. It is made from Rhine Riesling and the slight sweetness balances the natural high acidity of the Eden Valley Riesling. Eden Valley red wine is mainly a blend of Cabernet Sauvignon and Shiraz.

# 21

# The Barossa Valley Vintage Festival

WINEMAKING should be an enjoyable business. Wine is made to give pleasure to all kinds of people, and it is only fitting that the harvest of the vine should be an occasion for celebration. Grape and wine festivals are common in Europe and are an essential part of the wine scene. They are hallowed by tradition and are usually associated with feast days or other religious observances. The Barossa Valley Vintage Festival was clearly based on the famous German wine festivals and adapted to the Australian temperament and the Barossa Valley climate.

The first festival was held in 1948 and festivals are now staged every two years on the odd-numbered year. The atmosphere of the festival is carnival, with processions, dancing, music, song, feasting, wine drinking, grape picking contests and winery inspections. Whilst the tone of the festival is basically German in an Australian setting, many other ethnic groups contribute to its success. A number of national dancing groups exist in South Australia and these are regular and popular performers at the festival.

The organization of the festival is a mammoth task and is largely in the hands of local people. Over the years many of the prominent wine men and women in the Valley have given much of their time to the festival, at that stage of the year—vintage—when time is at a premium. Wine people occupying important positions in the 1971 Festival include George Kolarovich (president), Peter Lehmann and Bruce

Bottled wine storage at Yalumba, with Alfred Wark in the background

Treading the grapes at the 1971 Barossa Valley Vintage Festival

Brandy and spirit distillation is a complicated business

Wine in casks at a Valley winery

## THE BAROSSA VALLEY VINTAGE FESTIVAL

Hoffmann (vice-presidents), Colin Gramp (catering), Mrs Laurel Hoffmann M.B.E. (Vintage Queen competition), John Hill Smith (art exhibition), Tom Morris (Weingarten) and his capable wife Daphne (secretary-treasurer). They have the assistance and support of many other people in the Valley. Outside organizations such as Qantas and Trans-Australia Airlines also co-operate with the Festival Association. The aim of the festival is indeed a worthy one since the proceeds from all the activities are for district charities. Over $3000 was donated to these charities after the 1969 Festival.

The festival programme is always exciting and includes something for everyone. Among the regular functions are wine tastings and winery inspections, an art exhibition at Angaston, a wine auction of rare and outstanding wines, the Weingarten (an informal vintage dinner for more than 1200 people in a pavilion at Tanunda), performances of the Tanunda Liedertafel Choral Society, a street carnival at Nuriootpa, a Vintage Ball at Tanunda, a grape-picking championship at Angaston, a float parade from Nuriootpa to Tanunda, a Village Fair at Tanunda and the crowning of the Vintage Queen.

Each year the festival has special attractions, such as the visit in 1969 of the German Rhine Wine Queen, a young and delightful blonde girl named Heidrun Reim, whose parents own a family winery in Mussbach near Neustadt in West Germany. A return visit was arranged for the Barossa Vintage Queen Suzanne Hage, who made a whirlwind visit to Germany later in the year. Suzanne came from Bethany near Tanunda, one of the hamlets of historical importance.

One of the successes of the 1969 Festival was the President's Reception in the Kaiser Stuhl champagne cellar, where a luncheon was served for 250 people, including federal, state and wine industry dignitaries. The wine auction was another remarkable event in which some wonderful old wines were auctioned for, in some instances, some wonderful old prices. Keith Waterman paid $20 a bottle for Seppelt's 1895 Barossa Port; Max Lake paid $18 a bottle for some Hunter wines, and Frank Sheppard of wine tanker fame paid $8 each for six bottles of Yalumba 1929 claret, which was considered to be the best buy of the sale. Peter Lehmann and Ian Bruce, the auctioneers, were well rewarded for their efforts, which yielded no less than $10,924. The pre-auction dinner yielded $2700 and the whole Festival grossed $30,000. The Barossa Valley Vintage Festival is here to stay, as long as people like good wine, good entertainment—and the Barossa Valley.

# 22
# Miscellany

On the western outskirts of Tanunda are several small wineries: the Veritas winery of R. H. Binder Pty Ltd, and the Paradale and Arrawarra wineries. The latter two are now operated by Bernkastel Wines Pty Ltd. Paradale winery was formerly owned by the late Arthur Hanisch and Arrawarra winery by Mr and Mrs Dyer, and before that by J. F. W. Petras. It was founded by Petras's father in 1879. Bilyara winery is another small one, situated on Sturt Highway about two-and-a-half miles north of Nuriootpa. In 1969, Ken Kies established a winery called 'Karrawirra' near his seventy acre vineyard a few miles south of Lyndoch. 'Karrawirra' is an aboriginal name for a forest of red gums. Ken, one of the largest grapegrowers in the district, also played Australian Rules Football for West Adelaide. He markets regional wines and his winery overlooks the Valley.

Douglas A. Tolley Pty Ltd have an attractive vineyard called 'Medlands Estate' at Dorrien, and their small winery lies just south of the road to Seppeltsfield in a valley concealed from the road. It is quite old and serves as a fermenting cellar only; the wines are then sent to the company's main winery at Hope Valley near Adelaide for maturing and bottling.

A short distance south of Lyndoch is a winery which was formerly owned by Walter Reynell & Sons Pty Ltd of Reynella. It has not been in use for some years, except as a storage cellar for other wineries in the Valley. A short distance further south is Kelly's cellar which is now operated as a storage cellar by Orlando. Brian Chatterton and his brother established a small winery near Lyndoch in 1969.

One company which does not make wine but is closely associated with the wineries in the Valley is Tarac in Nuriootpa, situated just west of Kaiser Stuhl. Tarac is an organization which recovers winery wastes and is probably unique in the world. The company is involved in spirit recovery from grape skins or marc (pomace in California); it also distils under contract and recovers potassium bitartrate and grape seed oil. Tarac was founded in 1930 by a man of great foresight and ability, Mr A. J. Allen, now living in Adelaide. Tarac may be regarded as a service company, performing what has come to be an essential service to the wineries in the Valley and other winemaking areas. The techniques of product recovery used at Tarac were largely evolved by Mr Allen and his staff. The plant is managed by Max Hackett, who has a hard-working team—Reg Rankin the secretary, Graham Anderson the chief chemist, Stan Obst the production superintendent and Bob Rex the plant engineer—who have coped with very rapid expansion in recent years. A branch has been operating at Berri on the River Murray for some years, and a new branch has recently been opened at Griffith in New South Wales.

The Valley is changing over the years, particularly with an awakening of interest in tourism and an awareness that the ethnic, scenic and oenological attractions of the Valley could well be publicized more. The Barossa Valley Vintage Festival is having a great impact and new dining and accommodation facilities have recently appeared. '*Die Weinstube*' restaurant at Dorrien is very popular and Hermann Thumm's thirty unit Barossa Motel near Lyndoch is making a big contribution. Its dining room offers a sweeping view of the Lyndoch end of the Valley. A new motel 'The Vineyards Motel' has recently been built just east of the Vintners Co. Pty Ltd between Nuriootpa and

Angaston. The Nuriootpa Community Hotel, the Vine Inn, has added a large grill room on the northern side of the hotel. One man who has done much to publicize the wines of the Valley is Frank Nicholls of the Angaston Hotel. He has been a courteous 'mine host' to many visitors to the Barossa. Something new is on the way—Gramp's *'Weinkeller'* restaurant at Jacob's Creek between Rowland Flat and Tanunda in the ancestral home of the Gramp family. Knowing the thoroughness of Colin Gramp, this should be worth waiting for. There is something particularly enjoyable about eating and drinking in a vineyard, particularly if the wine comes from the same vineyard.

# 23
# Wine Types

THE Barossa produces a number of different types of wine, identified by an even greater number of names, many of which are unfamiliar outside the wine trade. It is understandable that the budding oenophile may be confused with terms which seem either synonymous or ambiguous, and some rationalization may be welcome.

In general, all wines may be classified into four main groups:

1. Appetizer wines—sherry (dry, medium and sweet) and flavoured wines, such as the vermouths.
2. Table wines—dry white (hock, chablis, white burgundy, riesling and other varietal wines); sweet white (moselle, graves, sauternes); dry red (claret, burgundy and varietal wines) and rosé wines.
3. Sparkling wines—champagne, sparkling burgundy, sparkling moselle, sparkling hock, sekt and pearl wines.
4. Dessert wines—port (ruby, tawny and vintage), muscat, marsala, madeira, tokay and others.

*Appetizer Wines*

Appetizer wines, such as sherry, are usually taken before a meal. If you are in an expansive mood, the ultimate in appetizers is champagne, particularly brut. Flor sherry will be discussed in a separate section. Its older and bigger brother is amontillado or medium sherry, usually

WINE TYPES

an old fino sherry which may have been sweetened somewhat. The best amontillados are dry. Sweet sherry and its near relative cream sherry are very popular wines and enjoy an enormous sale in Australia. They are all-purpose drinks, and can be mixed with lemonade or soda. Vermouths come in two basic styles: French which is dry and pale, and Italian which is sweet and dark. However, the Italians also make a French style and the French an Italian style, which makes it all rather confusing. The basis of all vermouths is a blend of selected herbs, which is added to a dry, acid, white wine for the French style, and to a sweet neutral dessert wine for the Italian style.

*White table wines*

White table wines come in a bewildering assortment of names and sweetness. In the past all white table wines, except sauternes, moselle and graves, were dry (less than one half per cent of sugar) but, with new techniques in the Barossa, it is possible to produce these wines with any desired amount of sugar. (All sugar comes from the grapes, by the way—by law no cane sugar can be added.) Some wines taste slightly sweet but in fact may be quite dry. An old matured white burgundy, for example, with a lot of flavour and fruit on the palate, may actually taste slightly sweet. The higher acid wines taste drier than those with low acid.

Generic names, such as hock, chablis, white burgundy, moselle, sauternes and graves, are still widely used in Australia. These names refer to wines which resemble those made in certain areas of France or Germany. In some cases the Australian counterpart may be very close to the European style, whilst in others the similarity may not be so clear-cut. Hocks are fresh, light, dry, flowery and fairly acid. Chablis styles (named after the town of Chablis in eastern France) are full-flavoured dry white wines, with a characteristic 'flinty' acid finish. White burgundies are rather like chablis, but are fuller, rounder and softer, with lower acidity. Moselles (more correctly 'Mosel', from the river which rises as the Moselle in north-eastern France and flows as the Mosel northwards through Germany) are similar to hocks but slightly sweet. Sauternes are distinctive wines which, apart from a few notable exceptions, Australians do not generally make very well. They are rich, fruity, golden, honey-like wines which should finish rather dry. Graves are slightly sweet white wines, rather rare in Australia. *'Graves'* means 'gravel' in French and is the name of a district with gravelly soils a few miles south of Bordeaux.

The opposite to generic or general names is varietal or specific names. A varietal name refers to the grape variety from which the wine was made. The practice of using varietal names is becoming more common in Australia, and is a means of naming wines which have distinctively recognizable flavours. Various varietal names are used in Barossa wines.

Riesling or Rhine Riesling is the famous white grape of the Rhine and one of the finest in the world. It has over twenty synonyms in various countries. The wine has a flowery nose and strong varietal character with a crisp acid finish. The grape is not a vigorous grower and the bunches are tight and subject to fungus diseases. The grapes do not have such a distinctive varietal character when grown in hot climates.

Hunter River Riesling or Sémillon is one of the famous grapes in the Graves and Sauternes areas of France. The wine is light, dry and delicate, with an acid finish and some varietal character. The grape is grown in the Riverina and Hunter River areas, as well as in the Barossa, and gives wines which are typical of these areas.

Clare Riesling is a variety which has caused considerable confusion. It was originally confused with Sémillon in the Barossa, but it is now clear that what was planted there as Sémillon is almost all Clare Riesling. The grape was brought to Clare from Austria last century and its

The late Fred Ludlow was at Salters for 63 years

Bacchus Club plaque at Salters

Cyril Henschke of
C. A. Henschke & Co., Keyneton

George Kolarovich of Kaiser Stuhl

Peter Lehmann of Salters

John Vickery of Château Leonay

name has been lost. It is not Riesling and is not related to it, but it makes some fine fruity wines nevertheless.

White Hermitage is a variety which rejoices in several names in other areas of Australia, such as Trebbiano (its Italian name), Ugni Blanc (one of its French names), White Shiraz, and in the Hunter Valley, Madeira. It is the cognac grape of the Charente in France, where it is known as St Emilion. The wine is pleasant, but rather neutral without much varietal flavour.

Tokay is a grape with a romantic name. It may be the Imperial Tokay or Harslevelü, or more likely Muscadelle. It makes a fragrant and fruity dry white wine and a fine dessert wine. Most of the plantings in South Australia are in the Barossa.

Verdelho is one of the grape varieties from Madeira; it makes a very distinctive wine, both table and dessert. The grape has a very fruity aromatic nose and a spicy and assertive flavour.

White Frontignac and Muscat Gordo Blanco are being used in the Barossa to produce delightful dessert wines and cream sherries, as well as table wines. The dry wines need to be very well made since they sometimes tend to coarseness. In 1964, the first new grape varieties in nearly seventy years were released in South Australia by the State Department of Agriculture. These varieties included Gewürztraminer and Sylvaner, and we will soon see wines made in the Barossa from these varieties. The Gewürztraminer, in particular, should be a winner.

*Red table wines*

Red table wines are frequently labelled as generic wines, either claret if they are firm, astringent and high in tannin, or burgundy if they are rounder, softer, fuller wines with less acidity. The claret style wines are frequently made from Shiraz and Cabernet Sauvignon and aged in small wood of either French or American oak. Burgundies also are usually made from Shiraz in the

Barossa, sometimes with Grenache and other varieties, and aged in large wood. Whilst we have the two generic names claret and burgundy, we also have various varietal names.

Shiraz or Hermitage is the same as the Syrah of the Rhone Valley and the Petite Sirah of California. It is the basis of most of the Australian dry red wines, and in the Barossa it produces a very fragrant wine with a deep purple colour when young. As far as I know, there is no variety in France called Hermitage, and Shiraz is called by this name in Australia because it is one of the dominant red varieties of the Hermitage district in the Rhone Valley.

When wine-lovers read 'Cabernet Sauvignon' on the label, they expect something good. Cabernet Sauvignon is one of the finest red wine grapes in the world. The great clarets from the Médoc, north-west of Bordeaux, all have some Cabernet Sauvignon in their make-up, and a fine claret tends to be synonymous with the Cabernet grape. Cabernet Sauvignon vines are one of the few vine varieties in the Barossa which can be recognized from a distance. The leaves appear to have holes in them, caused by the overlapping lobes. Like many good things in life, Cabernet Sauvignon grapes are hard to get. The yield is low, the bunches are small and furthermore, hard to pick. Setting is sometimes erratic and some bunches have tiny green immature berries. The berries are normally small and deeply coloured, with a pronounced varietal flavour. Because of all this the cost of Cabernet Sauvignon grapes is high, but they make wonderful wine.

Grenache is a good 'grower's' grape. It is easy to grow, fruits regularly and well, and is resistant to disease. The wine has a pleasant aromatic flavour with good acidity, but is generally low in tannin. Grenache is used for light dry red, as well as rosé, and also for tawny port and other dessert wines. It is often chosen as the blending wine with heavy and more robust types.

In the future, we will be seeing Pinot Noir and Gamay Beaujolais (actually a clone of Pinot Noir) on the labels of dry red wines. These varieties have only recently been released in South Australia, but they augur well for the future.

*Sparkling wines*

Champagne is the aristocrat of sparkling wines. It should be extremely delicate, clean and well-balanced, without too much varietal flavour. Champagne comes in a range of sweetness. *Brut* means dry or very nearly so; *sec* means slightly sweet, whilst *demisec* and *doux* are progressively sweeter. Sparkling hock and sparkling moselle are fuller flavoured wines and quite sweet. Sparkling burgundy is a light soft fragrant red wine with noticeable sweetness. Both sparkling burgundy and champagne can improve for a long time in bottle and the prizewinners are usually old wines. Cold Duck is a new arrival on the Australian scene; a bubbly red wine with a curiously catching name, which originated in the United States. Pearl wines are tremendously popular and the Barossa is the home of these wines. They have varying degrees of sweetness and may be white, pink or red. These wines have probably done more than any other to convert the non-winedrinker to an appreciation of wine.

*Dessert wines*

For many years, dessert wines were the mainstay of the Barossa and helped to establish the fame of the Valley. Dessert is an apt word, since many of these wines are drunk at the end of a meal. Dessert wines are sweet, usually low in acid and high in alcohol (grape spirit is added during the fermentation) and may be made from either red or white grapes.

Dessert wines made from red grapes comprise the ports, which come in three main styles—ruby, tawny and vintage. These wines are usually made from Shiraz,

Grenache, Mataro, and sometimes Cabernet Sauvignon. The best ports are matured in oak casks. When young, they have a deep ruby colour (hence the name ruby port), and develop into tawny ports with further wood ageing which lightens the colour. Vintage port is a high quality port of a particular year, aged in wood for eighteen months to two years, then matured for many years in bottle. These wines have a very deep full rich colour and a high tannin content, which forms a bottle crust with age.

There are two main muscat grapes which have a distinctive and unmistakeable flavour and produce wine which has possibly the most individual flavour of any wine. White muscat comes from the Gordo Blanco grape (Muscat of Alexandria, or Muscatel) and brown muscat comes from grapes of the Frontignac family (Muscat de Frontignan). The muscat dessert wines are very popular wines in Australia.

Other dessert wines are made in the Barossa from specific grapes whose names they bear, such as Tokay, Madeira, Sauvignon Blanc and other varieties. The wines are made in an identical manner and are usually aged in wood. Some of the finest old dessert wines in Australia are made in the Barossa.

# 24
# Technical Talk

THE interested wine-drinker frequently appreciates some technical details of the wines that he drinks. It gives him greater understanding of his wine and sometimes a little oneupmanship at the local Wine and Food dinner. Winemakers know this too, and many of them give little snippets of interesting technical information on the front or the back label.

It wasn't always so, however. One remembers the days when a bottle carried only the word 'claret' or 'hock', the maker's name, the contents of the bottle, and that was all. When we think about this, it is apparent that such labels do not really tell the drinker what is in the bottle. Many labels still don't, but the expressive and informative label does tell the customer what he is buying. Long may they continue!

Modern wine labels frequently tell the purchaser many things; which grapes the wine was made from, sometimes how ripe they were, how the grapes were handled, whether the fermenting wine was refrigerated, how it was aged and so on. The wine industry is moving fast in the technical sense and most of the new advances originate in the Barossa Valley. Without modern techniques, we could not be enjoying some of the wines now available. In this chapter, we are going to talk a little about these things.

*Fermentation*

All wines are the products of fermentation, a process which was known to the ancients, but has only been really thoroughly understood in the past thirty years. Fermentation is caused by yeasts, which were named before their precise nature was known. They were known by their action: causing dough to rise in breadmaking and producing bubbles in winemaking and brewing. So, not surprisingly, the name 'yeast' in various languages is related to its function. For example, *hefe* in German from *heben* to raise; *levure* in French from *lever* to lift or raise, and so on.

Fermentation is fantastically complicated. In 1815, Guy-Lussac set out the classical equation:

$$C_6H_{12}O_6 \rightarrow 2\ C_2H_5OH + 2\ CO_2$$
$$\text{glucose} \qquad \text{alcohol} \qquad \text{carbon dioxide}$$

This equation is nearly, but not quite, correct. It gives no indication of the complexity of the changes which take place between the disappearance of the sugar and the appearance of the alcohol and carbon dioxide.

Let us start from the beginning. The vines in the Barossa Valley, or anywhere else for that matter, use their canopy of green leaves to catch the energy from sunlight to form sugar (sucrose or cane sugar) by photosynthesis. This sugar is transported from the leaves to the grapes where it is broken down to grape sugar, which is a mixture of about equal proportions of glucose and fructose. As the grapes ripen in summer, the amount of sugar increases, whilst the amount of acid (mainly tartaric and malic acids) decreases. When the grapes are considered by the winemaker to be ripe, they are harvested and taken to the winery. Ripeness depends on the purpose for which the grapes are to be used. For example, if Riesling grapes are to be used for making delicate dry white wine, they will be picked rather early, when the baumé reading is about eleven degrees or sometimes less. If they are to be used to make a 'spätlese' or late-picked sweet table wine, they will be left to mature on the vine until they are fourteen degrees baumé or more.

Perhaps a word on units is appropriate here. The sugar content of the grape juice is usually measured by a hydrometer or refractometer. The hydrometer may be calibrated in degrees baumé, a table originally devised by Antoine Baumé in France for assessing the amount of salt in brine. It is a convenient scale, because one degree baumé produces approximately one per cent of alcohol by volume on fermentation. Alternatively the hydrometer may be calibrated in degrees brix or balling (these are synonymous) which corresponds to the concentration of cane sugar in water. The refractometer is calibrated directly in per cent sugar. Actually, measurements made with the baumé, brix or balling hydrometers or the refractometer do not give the exact amount of sugar in the grape juice. If we want to know exactly how much sugar is present we must measure this chemically. However, when the grapes are ripe the sugar content is far higher than the other dissolved solids and the hydrometer or refractometer is nearly correct if the result is regarded as representing only sugar.

Acidity is very important in grapes, since it adds balance to the wine. In general, the more acid it contains, the more the wine will benefit from ageing. The winemaker likes to know the acidity of the grape juice, and he measures this as titratable acidity, in terms of grams per litre as tartaric acid, or he may measure the pH, which is another expression of acidity or sourness, not directly related to titratable acidity. For white table wines, the winemaker likes his juice to contain between six and nine grams per litre of titratable acidity (which he sometimes calls total acidity). For dry red wines, he prefers the titratable acidity to be somewhat lower, as with dessert wines. The pH values do not have such a wide range. Almost all Australian wines lie in the pH range 3.0 to 4.3, the lower values applying to the more acid wines.

Let us return to the subject of fermentation. After the grapes are crushed and destemmed (and pressed, in the case of white wines) a pure yeast is usually added and fermentation begins. Sometimes the winemaker allows the fermentation to develop spontaneously, caused by the yeasts normally present on the surface of the grapes. This is less desirable, because the winemaker does not have much control over the types of yeasts which are present (except that given by sulphur dioxide) and off-flavours may develop.

The first change in fermentation is the formation by the yeast of a sugar phosphate ester, which is then broken down to two identical compounds, each half the size of the sugar molecule. Since sugar has six carbon atoms, these three carbon compounds undergo further changes until they release carbon dioxide, (which produces the bubbles during fermentation). Finally they form ethyl alcohol which contains two carbon atoms. Thus, two molecules of alcohol and two molecules of carbon dioxide are formed from each molecule of sugar. The complexity lies in the number of separate chemical changes which take place. There are no fewer than eleven separate reactions from sugar to alcohol, and twelve separate enzymes, together with several coenzymes and trace elements are involved.

One of the very important developments in winemaking in recent years is the widespread use of refrigeration for cooling the fermentation, and also for cold-stabilization of wine before bottling. The labels of many white wines state that the wine was refrigerated or cooled during fermentation, and in some cases the temperature range is given. The reason for cooling is that fermentation produces a great deal of heat which must be removed in some way, otherwise the wine will be flat and lacking in flavour. Refrigeration is the best way to keep fermentations cool, and the best dry white wines are fermented at about $55°$ to $60°F$. If cooling is not used the temperature could rise to $80°$ or $90°F$. or possibly higher, with a consequent reduction in quality of the wine. In this case we are speaking mainly of white wines. Red wines may be cooled a little but not usually as much as the whites. Many of the aroma and flavour compounds, which make wine what it is, are volatile (hence we can smell them). In hot fermentations these compounds are partly lost by being 'boiled' off and the wine is depleted of them.

Various other desirable compounds are formed during fermentation. Glycerine is one of these, and this exists in relatively high concentration in wine (between one-half and one per cent). Various acids such as lactic, succinic and acetic acids, are formed, as well as several higher alcohols; amyl, butyl and propyl. These are separated as fused oils, or tails, if the wine is distilled.

The number of chemical constituents found in wine is quite remarkable. The number at present stands at over 400, and the list is growing. These comprise alcohols, acids, esters, sugars, minerals and so on, and indicate the tremendous complexity of wine. We are now finding that our ideas about the compounds responsible for the taste of wine were very naïve. It is seldom the presence or absence of one compound which causes the difference in flavour and aroma between two sound wines. Rather, it is the complicated interaction of changes in concentration of many compounds. It is said that we only begin to learn when we realize how ignorant we are. Well, we are beginning to learn about wine flavour and aroma, but we still have a long way to go. Though the scientist has many complicated and expensive pieces of equipment to help him, in techniques such as gas chromatography, mass spectroscopy, spectrophotometry, and so on, the best equipment yet devised for assessing wine quality is the human nose and palate.

*Winemaking Processes*

The winemaking process consists of several phases, of which one is fermentation. When fermentation is complete (we are speaking here of table wines) and the last bubbles of carbon dioxide have been released, what happens next?

Let us first consider white table wines. The wine is cloudy because it contains suspended matter such as yeast cells, grape particles, bitartrate crystals and the like. This matter has been kept partly in suspension by the bubbles of carbon dioxide. The winemaker now needs to clarify the wine by racking (decanting) it from its yeast deposit, and then preventing oxidation by adding a measured amount of sulphur dioxide. When sulphur dioxide is added to wine, most of it is chemically bound to constituents in the wine, which effectively prevent it from exerting its germicide and antioxidant properties. The important portion of sulphur dioxide is that which remains free. In the past, winemakers measured only the total amount of sulphur dioxide present, but since this bore no simple relationship to the amount remaining free, the measurement was not very useful. Nowadays, the winemaker ensures (or should ensure) that the free sulphur dioxide is between approximately twenty and sixty parts per million for white table wines. One part per million isn't very much really—it is about one drop in ten gallons! But these parts per million are very important to the quality of the wine.

At this stage the wine is still somewhat hazy and needs to be clarified. This is done either by filtration, centrifugation or fining. All three of these procedures are used in the Barossa, but fining is still the most important at this stage. Several fining (clarifying) materials are currently in use, but the most important is bentonite, a white powder mined in various parts of the world. The bentonite used in Australia comes from the western United States, and is a hydrated aluminium silicate called montmorillonite (after Montmorillon in France, where it was first discovered). The bentonite is made into a thick suspension in a little hot water and mixed thoroughly with the wine, until the wine becomes quite hazy. But after a short time a curious thing happens. The haze coagulates into flocculent particles which settle to the bottom of the container, and the wine is left quite clear.

An equally curious and important event takes place during bentonite fining. Wines frequently contain a considerable amount of plant protein derived from the grape, and grape varieties differ widely in the amount of protein they contain. The muscats in particular contain a high level. If the wine is warmed by exposure to heat in a hot car or delivery truck, or in a hot shop window, protein may precipitate in the bottle as an unsightly haze, which alters the appearance of the wine but not its taste. In our present age of technology, a haze of this kind would not be accepted by the customer, so the winemaker needs to remove the protein before the wine is bottled. The surprising feature of bentonite fining is that not only does it clarify the wine, but it also removes the soluble protein, rendering the wine heat—or protein—stable.

The reason that bentonite removes protein is quite interesting. The bentonite particles are very tiny flat wafers with an enormous surface area covered with negative charges. The protein in wine is positively charged, and since positive and negative charges attract each other, bentonite binds the protein molecules and removes them from the wine. Some other absorptive and charge effects also take place, but this electrostatic removal is the most important mechanism.

The wine is now clarified and any future protein haze is prevented, but another factor still must be controlled. Wine is, among other things, a saturated solution of potassium bitartrate (cream of tartar) and when chilled, this compound may precipitate as crystals which, though harmless, are unsightly. So the winemaker chills the wine in bulk and potassium bitartrate precipitates as crystals, leaving the wine stable for further chilling. Potassium bitartrate crystals have some commercial value and they are sold in the form of argols to make cream of tartar, used in the kitchen. There are also other ways of stabilizing wine against potassium bitartrate crystallization, such as ion-exchange or the addition of a curious compound called metatartaric acid, which appears to sheath the tiny crystals and prevent them growing.

The wine is now ready for bottling and is given a polishing filtration to make it brilliantly clear. It is then bottled, capsuled and labelled. One of the great dangers of white winemaking in a hot area like the Barossa is oxidation, which results in lack of aroma and flavour, and darkening of colour. Several of the Barossa wineries are now preventing oxidation by adding a small quantity of ascorbic acid (vitamin C) to the wine which combines with oxygen, or by using inert gas, such as carbon dioxide or nitrogen, during handling and filling. The result of all these careful treatments, together with selection of the highest quality grapes, is that some of the premium Barossa white wines are the finest in Australia.

The procedure for making red table wines is somewhat different from those used for white table wines. The grapes are crushed and destemmed. Then they are fermented with a pure yeast in the presence of the grape skins from which the red colour is extracted. The skins are kept submerged in the fermenting juice by means of a 'false head', by plunging them below the surface of the juice, or by spraying the juice over the floating cap of skins.

When sufficient colour is extracted from the skins, they are pressed and removed, and the juice is allowed to ferment until all the sugar has disappeared. It is then racked (decanted) and placed in either oak or concrete containers to mature. Oak casks bring out the best in a red wine, and sometimes small casks of 60 or 120 gallons are used. The wine is racked several times and may be fined with bentonite, gelatin or white of egg. At one or two years of age, the wine is filtered and bottled, and may rest in bottle bins to mature in the bottle and build up its quality still further. One problem which the winemaker encounters with red wine is the strong consumer demand for quality wines. This is fine, but it means that the wines sometimes do not receive the length of maturation time which they require to develop their optimum quality. At present, it is difficult to find red wines older than about two to three years of age, and if the serious winebibber wants aged red wines, he really needs to buy them young and age them himself! A good dry red wine improves in bottle and may be kept five years or more with advantage.

The dessert wines, both white and red, are fermented off or on the grape skins, in more or less the same manner as for the table wines, except that skin contact is longer for white wines. The grapes are usually picked riper than for table wines, and at the right stage during fermentation, grape spirit (distilled from wine) is added to stop the fermentation and conserve the sugar in the wine. The wines are then racked, sulphur dioxide added, and bentonite clarification is carried out. When the wines are clarified, they are cold-stabilized and matured in wood or concrete. If the grapes are moderately high in acid (as well as sugar) they make wine which matures slowly and builds up wonderful flavour and aroma. The Barossa has many of these lovely old wines gently maturing in cool oak casks, and they are worth searching for. Most of the wineries have these special old dessert wines and they are relatively inexpensive when one considers the length of time they have been maturing.

*Flor Sherry*

The Sherry Party is an established part of Australian life, and a sherry (or two) before meals is an excellent relief from the cares of the day. Australian winemakers are adventurous souls. Name any type or style of wine and they will make it—with more or less success. When we consider that a winemaker in Germany, for example, makes usually only one kind of wine, the Australian winemaker shows a versatility that sets him apart. Sometimes, he is forced to make all types of wine, because his salesmen and agents demand it. If he does not offer the whole range, the agent or reseller may well go to the maker who can. This diversity of wines is commendable on the one hand, but undesirable on the other. If the winemaker could make all kinds of wine equally well (and some can) then nothing is lost, but the age of specialization requires that logically the winemaker should make those wines which his ability, his grapes and his facilities enable him to make best.

Flor sherry is a special case in which some Australian winemakers have shown a particular kind of expertise. The wine is hard to make, and the path to success is strewn with difficulties. But the best Australian sherries rate with the finest in the world. Spanish, South African and Australian flor sherries can be confused with each other in blind tastings. Besides the usual table and dessert wines, several wineries in the Valley, such as Yalumba, Seppelt's, Château Leonay and Gramp's, make excellent flor sherries. The average sherry drinker may not perhaps appreciate what this statement implies, and accordingly a few comments on sherries may not go amiss.

Fino or flor sherry derives its name from the Spanish. Sherry is a corruption of Jerez (actually Jerez-de-la-Frontera) a town in southern Spain not far inland from Cadiz. Jerez is the centre of the Spanish sherry industry. *Fino* means fine or high quality, and *flor* is the Spanish word meaning flower.

Flor sherry making is a complicated process involving secondary growth of a specially selected yeast under defined conditions. The base is a dry white wine made from rather acid grapes without pronounced varietal character, such as Pedro Ximenez or Palomino. The wine has to be made carefully, avoiding oxidation on the one hand and any more than minimum amounts of sulphur dioxide on the other, since the latter interferes with subsequent film growth of the yeast. The base wine is stabilized by fining and refrigeration. It is then lightly fortified with high-proof spirit to approximately fifteen per cent alcohol by volume (26 degrees proof spirit), and sterile-filtered into sterilized oak casks or covered concrete fermentation tanks. The wine is intentionally stored on ullage (a risky procedure), so that it presents a surface for inoculation with flor yeast (selected strains of *Saccharomyces*). The yeast grows on this surface and uses the air in the ullage space. The alcohol content at this stage is rather critical. If it is too low, the wine runs the risk of growing vinegar bacteria (*Acetobacter*), which turn it into vinegar. If it is too high, the flor yeast will not grow.

Provided the wine contains the correct amount of alcohol, no free sulphur dioxide, the temperature is right (16° to 21° Centigrade or 60° to 70° Fahrenheit is the optimum range), and the amount of aeration is right, the flor film will grow as a thin grey-green carpet over the wine. After the surface is covered with yeast, the flor character begins to develop, and one can smell the nutty sherry-like aroma above the film. Flor character is chemically very complex, but the level of acetaldehyde is a reasonable indication. During the flor stage, the winemaker takes regular measurements of acetaldehyde, which may rise from under fifty parts per million to over four hundred. The wine is taken off flor when the winemaker considers that it has sufficient flor character, usually eight to sixteen weeks in large tanks and one to three years or even longer in oak casks. It is then blended, filtered to remove the yeast, lightly fortified and put into oak casks for further ageing.

As we can see, the flor process is technically quite complicated, and while it constitutes an essential part of flor sherry making, it is not the only part. The winemaker needs to have patience (all good winemakers have this), a fine palate and good blending skill. Flor sherries are not made quickly and the finest in Australia are usually about three or four years of age when marketed. As the pale yellow fino sherries age, they become darker in colour and develop into amontillados, another Spanish term. These still retain the nutty, sharp sherry palate, and are usually sweetened a little to compensate for the rather bitter tannin acquired from prolonged wood ageing

Flor sherries in their natural state are quite dry and free from any fermentable sugar. They are the driest of the wines. The flor yeast sees to this. The finest finos are best drunk dry, but the fino sherries on the market are usually slightly sweetened to conform more to public taste. However those which win gold medals at wine shows are usually quite dry and high in flor character.

Sweet sherries on the other hand fall into two categories. Firstly there is the Australian sweet or cream sherry, usually a young fortified sweet wine made frequently from Muscat Gordo Blanco. Secondly there is the Australian oloroso (again a Spanish name), which is a sweetened flor sherry with plenty of wood age. The latter is a dark amber wine with strong sherry character, both rare and expensive.

Sherry flor yeast growing on wine is one of the most interesting and unusual features of winemaking. On first appearance, it is difficult to imagine the grey-green mould-like growth on top of the wine producing anything else but mouldy wine. But the proof of the pudding is, in this case, in the drinking! When next you are in a winery where flor sherry is being made, ask to see it. The winery may have a glass-ended cask on display, through which the film growth can be clearly seen. Australian winemakers are well-informed on flor sherry, due largely to the work of the late John Fornachon at the Australian Wine Research Institute in Adelaide.

When next you attend a sherry party, or have that sherry (or two) before dinner, it is worth recalling that you are drinking the end product of a complicated and precise winemaking process, which is successful only because certain strains of *Saccharomyces* yeasts form a stable film on the surface of wine after the primary fermentation.

Hoffmann's North Para winery

Hardy's Siegersdorf winery

Rovalley Wines at Rovalley Flat

A fully automatic grape press for making quality wine installed in a Barossa Valley winery

Automatic sterile bottling line at Gramp's Orlando winery

# 25
# Grapes in the Barossa

FROM the viewpoint of grapes, the Barossa and certain other parts of Australia are unusual. There are about 4000 recognizable varieties of grape vines in the world. They are all members of the *Vitis* genus, which has about thirty species. (The experts do not agree among themselves on the precise number.) Not all of them produce grapes, but one is pre-eminent—*Vitis vinifera*, which means 'wine bearing'. All the vines in the Barossa Valley (as in most vineyard areas of Australia) are *Vitis vinifera* growing on their own roots, a situation quite rare in the world of wine. In most parts of the world, *Vitis vinifera* grows as a grafted vine on the rootstock of another *Vitis* species. This is necessary to make it resistant to the vine louse, *Phylloxera*, which would otherwise kill the vine (if it were present). *Phylloxera* is not present in South Australia thanks to good Government quarantine and a deal of luck, and rootstocks are not needed, at least not for *Phylloxera*.

Some day, grapegrowers may wish to use selected rootstocks for other reasons, such as resistance to nematodes (eelworms) which debilitate the vines but do not kill them, or for drought resistance. Some of these rootstocks possess rather fancy names, such as 'Dogridge', 'Salt Creek' and 'AXRI'. We will not go further into rootstocks and *Phylloxera*, since they are not part of Barossa vines, but the spread of *Phylloxera* throughout the grapegrowing areas of the world makes fascinating reading for those who are interested.

Grapegrowing is expanding throughout Australia as a result of the current boom in table wines, and the statisticians predict that this expansion will continue. The 1970 vintage was the all-time record grape crop. No fewer than 350,000 tons were crushed for wine in Australia, of which 240,000 tons were crushed in South Australia, and 38,400 tons (sixteen per cent of the South Australian total) were grown and crushed in the Barossa Valley. Some other statistics are also interesting. For example, in March 1970, 63,000 acres of vines (nearly one hundred square miles) were growing in South Australia and eighty-nine per cent of them were used for wine. The interesting factor is the acreage not yet bearing (20,000), which shows the extent of expansion. In the Barossa Valley, there are 16,700 bearing acres and almost 4000 newly-planted acres which are not yet bearing. Details of the tonnage of the various varieties grown in the Barossa Valley are set out in the following table.

## GRAPES GROWN AND CRUSHED FOR WINEMAKING IN THE BAROSSA DISTRICT
### 1969-1970

| Variety | Bearing Acres | Not yet Bearing | Tons Crushed |
|---|---|---|---|
| Albillo (Sherry) | 375 | 12 | 667 |
| Cabernet Sauvignon | 182 | 248 | 270 |
| Cabernet Gros | 27 | 28 | 56 |
| Carignane | 338 | 38 | 725 |
| Currant | 97 | 3 | 73 |
| Doradillo | 1100 | 11 | 2353 |
| Frontignac | 332 | 2 | 734 |
| Grenache | 3294 | 793 | 8793 |
| Malbec | 18 | 45 | 26 |
| Mataro (Morrastel) | 1938 | 168 | 3175 |
| Muscat Gordo Blanco | 158 | 10 | 399 |
| Oeillade (Cinsaut) | 83 | 48 | 221 |

| | | | |
|---|---|---|---|
| Palomino ⎫<br>Pedro Ximenez ⎬<br>False Pedro ⎭ | 2231 | 168 | 6729 |
| Rhine Riesling ⎫<br>Clare Riesling ⎬<br>Sémillon<br>Madeira ⎭ | 1808 | 766 | 4291 |
| Sercial | 226 | 7 | 409 |
| Shiraz (Black Hermitage) | 2658 | 997 | 5320 |
| Tokay | 500 | 114 | 1036 |
| White Hermitage* | 522 | 38 | 1385 |
| Portugal | 19 | 55 | 67 |
| TOTAL | 16,700 | 3,660 | 38,410 |

*Also known as White Shiraz, Trebbiano and Ugni Blanc (Source—Commonwealth Bureau of Census and Statistics).

The figures in the columns of the table do not add up to the totals, because a few other varieties planted in very small acreages have been omitted. However the table gives some rather important information. The varieties which show the greatest potential increase, relative to the acreage bearing at present, are those destined for table wines, such as Cabernet Sauvignon, Grenache, Malbec, Riesling and Shiraz. It is unfortunate that the statistics do not separate Rhine Riesling from Clare Riesling, Semillon and Madeira. Recent plantings in this group are largely accounted for by increased planting of Rhine Riesling, mainly in Eden Valley and other areas in the Barossa Hills.

Grape-growers the world over show a notable lack of interest in the correct naming of the grape varieties they cultivate, and the Barossa vignerons have been true to type in this respect. Three distinct varieties have been grown under the name 'Riesling', although only one, the Riesling from the Rhine, can justly claim the name. The variety Sémillon, native of south-west France, is called 'Riesling' in the Hunter River district of New South Wales, and the name has been applied likewise in South Australia. But in a complex of errors a third variety, not yet identified with its origin in Europe, and called 'Clare Riesling' for the time being, was planted in the Barossa under the belief that it was Sémillon, and called 'Hunter River Riesling'! To complete the comedy, if the reader has not already lost himself in the maze of mistaken identities, a variety which has been grown in the Barossa since its beginning under the name Madeira, turns out to be Sémillon! The hapless statistician has no hope at present of separating these three varieties and their aliases.

The Barossa district has developed a reputation for quality wine, and the anticipated increase in the tonnage of grape varieties destined for quality table wines is safeguarding this image. An important principle is involved here. Unless dry-land wine-growing areas, with relatively low yields of grapes per acre, produce wines of quality to compensate for their low yield, they risk being eclipsed by the many good wines produced in the irrigation areas of the Murray and the Murrumbidgee Rivers. This applies to both dessert and table wines. Many of the dessert wines made in the irrigation areas from high yielding vines are inexpensive and of good quality, and the Barossa has wisely diverted an increasing amount of local grapes from dessert to table wines. This, of course, does not apply to the dessert wines which are made from irrigated grapes, which the Barossa wineries grow or purchase from the Murray Irrigation Area. In general terms, low-yielding vines produce grapes with more flavour than high-yielding vines. It is difficult to decide on an optimum yield beyond which quality is reduced, but the figure could be in the region of four to six tons per acre, depending on various factors, such as soil type and viticultural practice. Irrigation practised in various Barossa vineyards may, by preventing severe droughting, actually raise both the yield per acre and the quality of the grapes produced. The limiting factor here is the availability of water, which is expensive in the Barossa when compared with the river irrigation areas, and thus has to be used carefully.

The average yield of grapes per acre in the Barossa over the past twenty-one years is 1.65 tons, and figures range from 1.08 tons in 1960 to 2.16 tons in 1964. The yield per acre depends on the soil, the season's rainfall, viticultural practices and grape variety. Derek Smith of the Geography Department of the University of Adelaide found that the average yield on a sample of farms in the Barossa for the three years 1966-1969 was 1.37 tons per acre, and individual varieties ranged from 2.70 tons for Clare Riesling to 0.62 tons for Cabernet Sauvignon. Yield for Rhine Riesling was only 0.88 tons and for Shiraz, 1.51 tons.

In view of this low yield of quality wine grapes, there has to be some price differential. The minimum prices for wine grapes are fixed annually by the South Australian Prices Commissioner, and these prices are used as a basis for sale and purchase of grapes. Some examples of the minimum prices gazetted in 1971 for non-irrigated grapes (that is, grapes not grown in defined irrigation areas along the River Murray) are as follows:

| | |
|---|---|
| Cabernet Sauvignon | $130 per ton |
| Rhine Riesling | $115 ,, ,, |
| Shiraz | $104 ,, ,, |
| Malbec | $ 99 ,, ,, |
| Sémillon and Clare Riesling | $ 88 ,, ,, |
| Grenache and Mataro | $ 76 ,, ,, |
| Muscat Gordo | $ 68 ,, ,, |

In view of the low yield of some of the high quality varieties, many growers consider that the price differential is not sufficient to encourage them to plant these varieties. If this belief prevails, we could well see an increase in the relative prices of some of the highest quality varieties in the future.

# 26

# Climate of the Barossa

ONE of the most important factors influencing the quality of wine is the climate, particularly the temperature, of the area in which the grapes are grown. In some quality areas, the climate is the limiting factor. For example, if the season is not sufficiently warm in the wine-growing areas of Western Germany, the grapes will not ripen and the vintage will be poor, as happened in 1965. Since northern Europe is more or less on the limit of viticulture, the vintage year is very important and can be quite critical. The finest years in this region, as in much of Europe, are the warmest years. It is rare to have too much heat on the Rhine or the Mosel, but insufficient heat is common.

Climatologists have spent a great deal of time establishing what are called homoclimes, or different places on the earth's surface with the same or similar climate. Professor Prescott, the former Director of the Waite Agricultural Research Institute in Adelaide, has made a notable contribution to this field and has found that the Barossa Valley has no climatic counterpart in France or Germany. Its counterpart is closer to Portugal, where the Mediterranean climate (cool wet winters and hot dry summers) is similar.

Some years ago, I compared the climate records of a number of Australian and western European areas and found some interesting comparisons. The accompanying simplified table gives certain comparative data between

## CLIMATE OF THE BAROSSA

Nuriootpa, Geisenheim on the Rhine in Germany, and Bordeaux in France. Climate is a capricious term. It embraces temperature, rainfall, solar radiation, relative humidity, wind, frost, cloud cover and other features. The aspect of the vineyard (the direction it faces) may also be very important. One or two climatic features may be comparable; for example, Nuriootpa and Geisenheim in Germany have similar annual rainfall, but differ widely in various other aspects, including the monthly distribution of rainfall. Examination of the climatic data over the growing period of the vine (October to about March or April for the Barossa, depending on the grape variety, and May to October or November for parts of Europe) shows that the climate in the Barossa is hotter and drier than both of the European regions mentioned. This is characteristic of many viticultural areas in southern Australia. The Barossa is really rather an arid region in summer when the vines need water most. Consequently, irrigation over this period is desirable, and indeed, many vineyards in the Barossa nowadays receive some irrigation from wells or bores drilled for the purpose. This low summer rainfall is coupled with a high solar radiation and low relative humidity, meaning that the evaporation rate of water from the soil, from vine leaves and from lakes and streams is very high. As can be seen, the amount of solar radiation (measured as gram calories per square centimeter per day) received by the vines in the three areas listed is quite different.

Solar radiation has meaning in relation to vintage years. We all know how important are vintage years in European viticulture, and many oenophiles carry with them little wallet cards listing the vintage years in the various famous winegrowing areas in Europe. These little cards look very impressive and may be approximately true for the region in general, but individual differences in wines within any one region can be quite large. Statistics of this sort do not apply to the individual wine, only to the area in general. If

## WINES & WINERIES OF THE BAROSSA VALLEY

*Climatic comparison between the Barossa Valley (Nuriootpa), Geisenheim in the German Rheinland and Bordeaux in France*

### NURIOOTPA (34.5° South)

| Month | Rain (in.) | Mean Temperature | | | Relative Humidity % | Solar Radiation |
|---|---|---|---|---|---|---|
| | | Min. | Av. | Max. | | |
| Jan. | 0.8 | 55 | 69 | 83 | 40 | 610 |
| Feb. | 0.9 | 56 | 69 | 83 | 42 | 505 |
| Mar. | 0.8 | 53 | 66 | 78 | 44 | 390 |
| April | 1.2 | 49 | 59 | 70 | 53 | 325 |
| May | 2.3 | 43 | 53 | 62 | 67 | 235 |
| June | 2.4 | 43 | 51 | 58 | 70 | 200 |
| July | 2.3 | 40 | 47 | 55 | 75 | 190 |
| Aug. | 2.8 | 40 | 48 | 57 | 72 | 275 |
| Sept. | 2.4 | 41 | 52 | 62 | 61 | 335 |
| Oct. | 1.6 | 46 | 56 | 67 | 53 | 475 |
| Nov. | 1.2 | 47 | 60 | 72 | 43 | 565 |
| Dec. | 1.2 | 52 | 65 | 80 | 39 | 600 |
| Total | 19.9 | — | — | — | — | 4705 |
| Mean | — | 47 | 58 | 69 | 55 | — |

### RHEINGAU (Geisenheim, W. Germany 50.0° North)

| Jan. | 1.4 | 28 | 33 | 38 | 85 | 75 |
|---|---|---|---|---|---|---|
| Feb. | 1.3 | 29 | 36 | 42 | 80 | 130 |
| Mar. | 1.3 | 33 | 42 | 50 | 74 | 225 |
| April | 1.4 | 40 | 49 | 59 | 68 | 335 |
| May | 1.6 | 47 | 57 | 68 | 68 | 450 |
| June | 2.1 | 52 | 63 | 74 | 68 | 485 |
| July | 2.1 | 55 | 65 | 76 | 71 | 490 |
| Aug. | 2.1 | 54 | 63 | 75 | 74 | 360 |
| Sept. | 1.8 | 49 | 59 | 69 | 79 | 290 |
| Oct. | 2.0 | 42 | 49 | 57 | 83 | 155 |
| Nov. | 1.6 | 35 | 40 | 45 | 85 | 85 |
| Dec. | 1.7 | 30 | 35 | 40 | 86 | 50 |
| Total | 20.1 | — | — | — | — | 3130 |
| Mean | — | 41 | 49 | 58 | 77 | — |

Quality control laboratory at Penfold's, Nuriootpa

Science and technology have an important role—pressure tanks at Gramp's Orlando Winery

## BORDEAUX, France (44.8° North)

| | | | | | | |
|---|---|---|---|---|---|---|
| Jan. | 3.1 | 35 | 42 | 49 | — | 125 |
| Feb. | 2.8 | 36 | 44 | 52 | — | 180 |
| Mar. | 2.4 | 40 | 49 | 59 | — | 350 |
| April | 2.2 | 44 | 54 | 64 | — | 350 |
| May | 2.5 | 49 | 59 | 69 | — | 480 |
| June | 2.4 | 55 | 65 | 76 | — | 525 |
| July | 2.0 | 57 | 68 | 79 | — | 570 |
| Aug. | 2.4 | 57 | 68 | 79 | — | 425 |
| Sept. | 2.7 | 54 | 65 | 75 | — | 325 |
| Oct. | 2.9 | 47 | 57 | 66 | — | 230 |
| Nov. | 4.0 | 41 | 49 | 56 | — | 130 |
| Dec. | 3.6 | 36 | 43 | 49 | — | 115 |
| Total | 33.0 | — | — | — | — | 3805 |
| Mean | — | 46 | 55 | 64 | — | — |

you want to try a little oneupmanship, carry one of these cards with you. You don't have to use it; just carry and occasionally display it with a knowing air!

Sometimes the season in parts of Europe is so bad that the winery may not offer any wine for sale under its usual label. In the Barossa, vintage years do differ in a relatively minor way, but not with such drastic fluctuations. In recent years, 1968 and 1969 were somewhat poorer years than usual for red wines because of poor ripening conditions and rain at harvest. The result was that the colour in red wines was somewhat lighter. In 1970, however, the crop of grapes and their quality were very good indeed, and some very excellent wines were made.

The climate in the Barossa is not uniform. In the Valley itself, the yield of grapes is greater in the southern end near Lyndoch, where the rainfall is higher. On the western rim where the rainfall tends to be lower, near Greenock and Seppeltsfield, the yield is also depressed, and in places may be uneconomical. The Valley's average yield of grapes is 1.65 tons to the acre (450 to 600 vines), and the range of yields per acre is from less than one ton to about eight tons in a few vineyards near Lyndoch.

The Barossa Hills, including Eden Valley, Springton and Pewsey Vale, are cooler than the Valley proper. When Wally Boehm was the State Viticulturalist in the Department of Agriculture, he made some detailed temperature measurements, which showed that the Hills are significantly cooler than the Valley and ripening is delayed by about three weeks. The average temperature during the growing period of the vine is almost 3°F. lower in the Hills. In general terms, and with a few exceptions, the best wines are grown in the Barossa Hills and the slopes leading to them, rather than in the Valley itself.

Rainfall in the Barossa varies from about eighteen inches per year on the western side to thirty inches in the hills near Pewsey Vale. Some figures illustrate the extent of these differences:

|  |  |
|---|---|
| Gawler | 17.8 inches |
| Nuriootpa | 19.9 ,, |
| Tanunda | 21.2 ,, |
| Keyneton | 21.5 ,, |
| Lyndoch | 22.7 ,, |
| Williamstown | 25.9 ,, |
| Pewsey Vale | 30.5 ,, |

As one moves westwards from Eden Valley up into the hills, the annual rainfall increases rapidly, and in a distance of about one mile, increases from twenty-two to thirty inches. The highest point is Pewsey Vale Peak, 2064 feet, compared with Tanunda 864 feet, and Lyndoch 595 feet.

Some of the early explorers considered that the Valley would yield a vast quantity of underground water, but this opinion has not been substantiated. Underground water is difficult to find outside the Lights Pass area, and carries a high level of dissolved salts. It is nevertheless valued wherever it is found. For production of the grape crop, growers must rely mainly on winter rains stored in the top three to six feet of the soil. Some vine roots may be found down as far as twenty feet or more, but they are so few that they can make no substantial contribution to grape production. In an average vineyard, eighty to ninety per cent of the vine roots grow in the first two or three feet of the soil, so it is mainly on this thin mantle that the vines depend for their season's growth. Vines commonly show signs of water stress (dull green colour and some leaf drop) during the summer, the severity depending on the depth of the soil and its capacity to store water. (Clays hold much more water than sands.)

One of the problems in the Barossa is that rain falls mainly in the winter months, and the vines are limited during the growing season for lack of water, particularly from November onwards. In fact, there is a serious water deficit in summer caused by strong evaporation amounting to about five inches from a free water surface. In this situation, vines will respond to irrigation, both in yield and quality of the fruit. All of this indicates that the Barossa, like most of South Australia, is a semi-arid area. The greenness of the vines in summer tends to belie this, but the climatic records tell the story.

# 27

# Soils in the Barossa

THE Barossa Valley and the Barossa Hills are geologically very old. Earth fracture formed a valley, which at its lowest point served as a water course—the North Para River. For centuries, the rains have soaked the hills and run off down to the valley to flow into the river, and thence out to sea. The water washed rock particles from the hills to partially fill the valley, and on the basis of this transported material a variety of soil types have formed.

In describing soils, it is necessary to look not only at what we see on the surface but also at what lies below, because it is here that the vine roots draw their nourishment. The soil expert equips himself with a post-hole borer to obtain a profile of the soil and a measurement of the thickness of various layers. If you are interested in what lies below the surface of the soil, but do not have a post-hole borer or a shovel, examine railway or road cuttings. If these are recently made, the soil profile usually stands out clearly. Soil appearance in profile can be fascinating.

The most fertile soils are rich red-brown earths. They foster growth of vines and various other vegetable crops, which comprise the agriculture of the Valley. These soils consist of a top layer of brown to grey-brown sandy loam up to two feet deep over a red-brown clay which contains a varying amount of lime.

Whilst many soil types are found in the Valley, the other soil present in greatest quantity is solodized solonetz (a Russian term). This consists of light grey to grey-brown top soil sharply divided from a mottled yellow-brown or grey subsoil, having a curious columnar structure and also containing limestone. This soil is common to the Vine Vale area and though less fertile than the red-brown earths, it is still quite satisfactory for vineyards.

Terra rossa soils exist in patches in the Valley, particularly near Lyndoch. They are red-brown sandy loams about six to twelve inches deep often overlying limestone. Rendzina soils are also present and are similar to terra rossa, except that the surface is dark grey.

In the Eden Valley-Springton area, the soils belong to a distinctly different group in that they show an acid reaction throughout the profile. The parent rocks (micaceous schist and granite) sometimes protrude above the surface as rocky outcrops. The soils are podzols and are divided into yellow and grey-brown after the colour of the subsoil. Podzols consist of grey-brown loamy sands from six to eighteen inches deep overlying yellow to grey-brown clay above the parent rocks below. The area is very hilly and rain over the centuries has washed some of the soils down into Flaxman's Valley to form small alluvial flats. Various minerals exist in this area, such as asbestos, talc and copper, which have been mined from time to time. There is also some very good marble in the area, and a cement works which mines limestone is situated just west of Angaston.

# 28

# Grape and Wine Research in the Barossa

In any field of agriculture, it is important and sometimes essential to carry out research to improve yield or quality, and to prevent pests and diseases from attacking the crop. Such research is as important with grapes as it is with other agricultural crops, and since 1938 the South Australian Department of Agriculture has operated a viticultural research station in the Valley about two miles east of Nuriootpa.

The research station covers fifty acres (forty-five planted with vines.) It is concerned with carrying out research on grape varieties, methods of pruning, trellising, fertilizing, pests and diseases, and so on. Over the years, a great deal of information has accumulated on these subjects, and this is made available to grape growers at field days, as well as being reported in publications produced by the Department. Considerable work has been carried out on vine-bud mite and methods of overcoming vine disorders. The station also makes regular meteorological measurements.

Harry Tulloch was manager for some years before he left to enter private industry, and his place was taken by Max Loder, an entomologist from Freiburg in southern Germany. Recently Reg Radford has been appointed manager leaving Max Loder free to continue his work on vine mites. During this period, Wally Boehm was involved with the station in his capacity as State Viticulturist, and the Australian Wine Research Institute in Adelaide has been fortunate in being able to use some of the grapes for experimental winemaking. Some grapes have also gone to Roseworthy Agricultural College for teaching purposes in the winemaking course offered by the College. A notable success at the station has been the demonstration of a response to superphosphate in grapevines. The experiment is notable because in world-wide experience vines had not previously shown any benefit from this fertilizer.

The Barossa grapegrower is basically a practical man. Whilst he may be impressed and possibly bewildered by some of the modern scientific equipment and facilities, he still wants to know what all of this is doing for him. This is indeed a reasonable question which should also be directed at agricultural research generally. The field days at the Nuriootpa Viticultural Research Station are an education in several ways. The growers are usually very interested and sympathetic with the work which the researchers are doing, but the researchers must be able to talk to the grower in terms which he understands. The Department of Agriculture staff seem to do this very well. They see the need for proper communication and are trained for it.

In 1966, 200 grapegrowers banded together on a voluntary basis under the aegis of the Department of Agriculture to form something new and important, the Barossa Vine Selection Society. They select the best vines from their vineyards and have now established 200 clones (pure lines) from six quality grape varieties which serve as selected vines for new vineyards in the Valley. In addition, the Department of Agriculture has introduced, tested and released fourteen grape varieties which will influence the wine which we will see from the Barossa in the future. We can expect some fine wines from Gewürztraminer, Pinot Noir, Merlot, Sylvaner and other varieties.

From the winemakers' point of view, there is frequently an unanswered question in much of the research on grape vines. The usual, and sometimes the only measurement made following various viticultural experiments, such as pruning, fertilizing and so on, is measurement of the yield of grapes obtained. This is fine as far as it goes, but what kind of wine do the grapes make? In viticultural research in Australia, this question is now being asked more urgently, and it is to be hoped that the wine researchers and the grape researchers will integrate their results. It is not only important to know that a particular type of trellis yields more grapes, but also that the grapes are suitable for making good wine.

The Division of Horticultural Research of C.S.I.R.O. in Adelaide and in Merbein, northwest Victoria, is carrying out some very interesting work on grape crop predictions in addition to other viticultural research. This work is sponsored by the Australian Wine Board and follows the successful work carried out by the Division with sultana grapes in the Sunraysia area around Mildura. A reliable predicting service for wine grapes in the Barossa and elsewhere could be of much use to both the grapegrowers and the winemakers. It could inform them ahead of time of the grape yields which they could anticipate and enable them to plan ahead.

Many people discuss and speculate on the relative importance of soil type, climate and grape variety on wine quality, particularly table wines. The Australian Wine Research Institute has been involved in research on this subject in the Barossa for six years, in conjunction with the State Department of Agriculture, the C.S.I.R.O. Division of Soils and the Commonwealth Bureau of Meteorology. Many of the grapegrowers in the Valley co-operated in this large experiment and were most helpful in making measurements and helping to record data.

The experiment involved a great deal of work and produced some very interesting results. In the Barossa and Eden Valleys, the most important factor influencing wine quality was the variety of grape used. (All wines were made by a carefully standardized and replicated technique). Next came the climate and last and least of all was soil type. All grapegrowers know that the yield of grapes is affected by soil, climate and grape variety. They know that certain parts of their vineyard grow more grapes than others. What this experiment has shown is that these differences in yield are not related to quality of the wine made, at least as far as the trial plots in the Barossa are concerned. Even with grapes of the same variety grown on two very different soils—red-brown earth and solodized solonetz in the same locality—the quality of the wines made was indistinguishable. It is refreshing to be an iconoclast once in a while.

# 29
# The Future

THE future of the Barossa seems assured. The quality of the wines being made in the Valley is better than at any time in its history. The fine white and red wines of the Barossa and Eden Valleys are in world class, and as both grapegrowing and winemaking practices improve with advancing technology, so may we expect further improvement in the quality of the wines.

The future seems assured for another reason—tourism. The Valley is unique in Australia for its cultural heritage, some of its scenery, its oenological attractions and some of its foods. The tourist potential is only beginning to be appreciated, and as people travel more, we can expect to see tourism in the Valley flourish far beyond its present level. More needs to be done to foster tourism. There is a need for more first-class accommodation and dining facilities in settings appropriate to the Valley—preferably in a vineyard with a vista of the vines. To eat the foods and drink the wines of the Valley in such surroundings is in itself a delight and an experience. This can be coupled with visits to wineries (some of which could do much more to encourage tourists) and with properly-presented displays of the culture and background of the Valley. The Barossa has so much to offer the sightseer, but foresight and enthusiasm are needed to present the Barossa to the public in a way in which it will display its real merits.

One final note—the wines of the Valley need no bush. They can be offered and drunk with enjoyment and pride, and the wines, the winemakers and their wineries, make a contribution of increasing significance to our way of life.

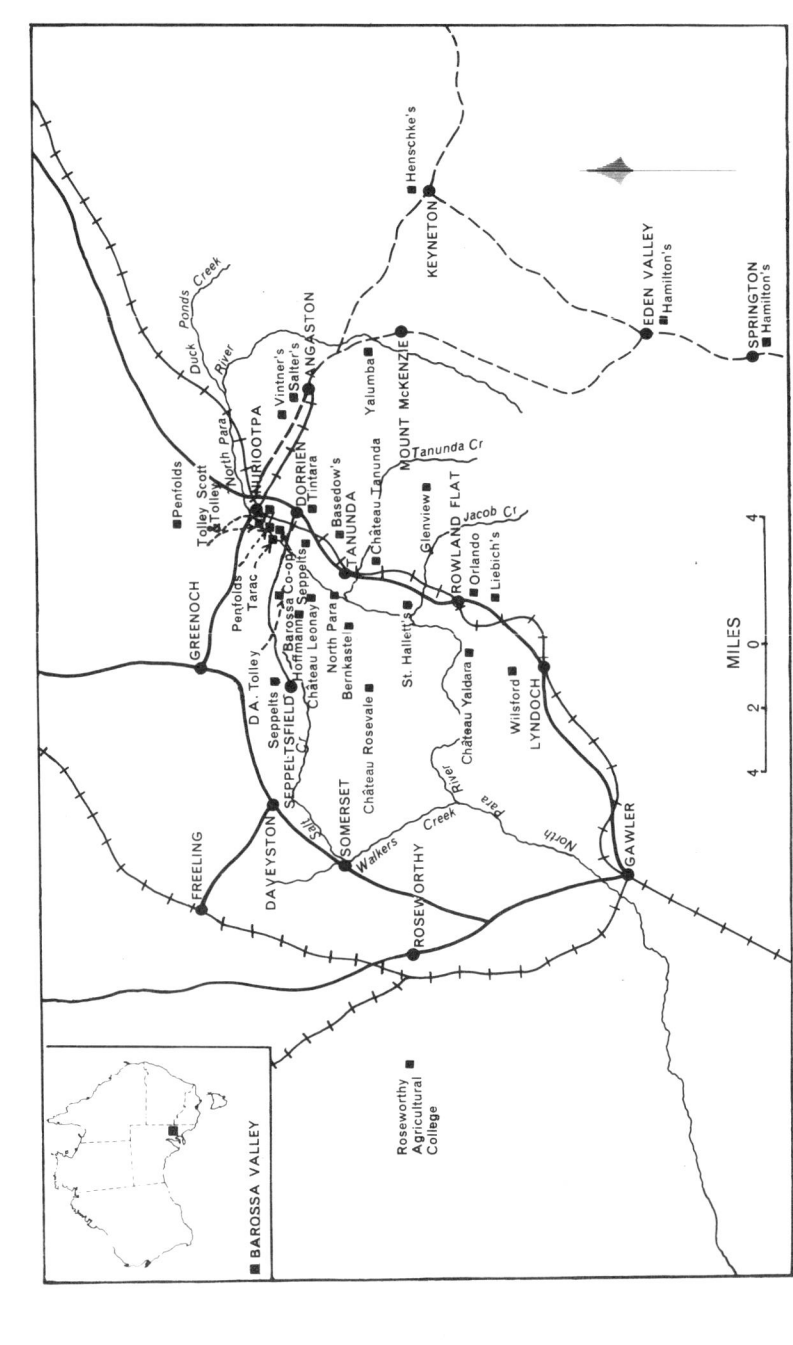

# Index

**A**

Aborigines 2
acetaldehyde 83
acetic acid 77
*Acetobacter* 83
acid finish 67
acidity 75
Ackland, Lance 39
Adelaide 1, 6, 9, 13, 57, 63, 64, 84, 90
Adelaide Bacchus Club 28
Adelaide Wine Show 52
aerated waters 14
aeration 83
air-bag press 42
Alameda Tawny Port 30
Albillo 29, 86
Aldgate 6
Alexandria 72
Allan, Malcolm 43
Allen, A. J. 64
Alsace 54
American oak 69
Amontillado 21, 66, 67, 83
amyl alcohol 77
Anderson, Graham 64
Angas, George Fife 2, 3, 19
Angas Park 3
Angaston 3-5, 19, 20, 24, 30, 31, 61, 65, 97

Angaston Hotel 65
Angas Town 3
anti-oxidant 78
appetizer wines 66-7
apple wine 30
argols 79
Arrawarra winery 63
art exhibition 61
artificial innoculation 16
ascorbic acid 80
aspect 91
auslese 15, 16
Australian Burgundy 26
Australian Wine Board 10, 29, 100
Australian Wine Research Institute 84, 100
Austria 68
automatic bottling lines 37
automatic horizontal press 37

**B**

Bacchus Club 27
Bad Kreuznach 16
Baldwin, Richard 43
balling 75
Barmeja Peninsula 2
Barossa Cabernet 17
Barossa Co-operative Winery Ltd. 34-38

105

Barossa Deutsche 4
Barossa Hills 1, 5, 22, 87, 94, 96
Barossa Motel 53, 64
Barossa Pearl 12-14
Barossa Reservoir 6
Barossa Riesling 12-14, 22
Barossa Valley Vintage Festival 60-62, 64
Barossa Vine Selection Society 99
Barrosa 2
Basedow, John 45
Basedow's Wines 45
baumé 25, 74, 75
Baumé, Antoine 75
Bavaria 12
Beckwith, Ray 26, 27
*Beeren auslese* 16
Bell, Mel 8
Bendigo 19
bentonite 78-81
Bernkastel Wines Pty Ltd 63
Berri 64
Bethany 3, 4, 32, 47, 61
Bilyara 5
Bilyara winery 63
Binder, R. H., Pty Ltd 63
Bird Cage 25
Birdwood 6
bitartrate crystals 78
Black Hermitage 87
Blass, Wolfgang 39, 40
Boehm, Wally 94, 98
Bordeaux 68, 70, 91-93
*Botrytis cinerea* 15, 16
bottle crust 72
brandy spirit 21
brix 75
brown muscat 72
Bruce, Ian 62
*brut* 71
brut champagne 66
Burge family 56
Burgoynes 26

burgundy 66, 69, 70
Buring, Leo 41-43
Burnside 29
Burra 6
Burton, Ron 57
butyl alcohol 77

C

Cabernet 16, 45
Cabernet Gros 86
Cabernet Sauvignon 17, 22, 29, 30, 56, 58, 59, 69, 70, 72, 86, 87, 89
Cadiz 2, 82
California 16, 26, 64, 70
cane sugar 67, 74, 75
carbonated wines 14
carbon dioxide 13, 15, 74, 76-78, 80
Carignane 86
Carte d'Or 22
Cartwright, Bob 37
centrifugation 78
centrifuge 15, 37
Chablis 66, 67
Chain of Ponds 5
Chamber of Manufacturers of S.A. 10
Champagne 14, 15, 61, 66, 71
Championship Show Fino 21
Charente 69
Charmane 52
Château Leonay 41-44, 82
Château Rosevale 57
Château Tanunda 8-11
Château Yaldara 53
Chatterton, Brian 64
Chiquita Sherry 21
Cinsaut 86
Clare Riesling 29, 30, 51, 56, 68, 86, 88, 89
claret 66, 69, 70, 73

# INDEX

clarifying 78, 81
*Classic wines of Australia* 22
climate 90-95, 101
clone 71, 99
cloud cover 91
co-enzymes 76
Cognac grape 69
Cold Duck 71
cold-stabilization 76, 81
Commonwealth Export Development Council 10
controlled cold fermentation 30
controlled environment 16
Coonawarra 22
Coulthard, William 3
cream sherry 67, 69, 84
currant 86

D

Davenport, John 35
Daveyston 6
Deboy, Hermann 54
decanting 78, 80
*demisec* 71
Depression 34
dessert wines 66, 71-72, 88
Die Weinstube 7, 35, 64
Director's Special Port 21
Distillers Co. Ltd 39
Dogridge 85
Dolan, Bryon 29, 30
Dolcetto 21
Doradillo 86
Dorrien 5, 7, 8, 35, 50, 63, 64
*doux* 71
Dyer 63

E

Ebenezer 4
*Edelfäule* 15, 16
Eden Moselle 51
Eden Valley 1, 5, 6, 18, 31, 36, 39, 50, 57, 87, 94, 97, 100, 102
Eden Valley Riesling 26, 59

Eden Valley Wines & Vineyards Pty Ltd 58
Eichig 12
Elizabeth 6
English colonists 3
enzymes 76
esters 21, 77
ethyl alcohol 77
European climate 15
Ewell Vineyards 58

F

Falkenberg, Brian 37
Falkenberg, P. T., Ltd 49
false head 80
False Pedro 87
Fanto, John 50
Faseth, Hubert 37
Federal Viticultural Council 13
Federal Wine & Brandy Producers Council 10
fermentation 8, 13, 14, 37, 71, 73-77, 81
fertilizing 98, 100
Festival Association 61
filtration 78
fining 78, 79, 82
fino sherries 21, 67, 82-84
First World War 4, 35, 58
Flaxman, Charles 3
Flaxman's Valley 97
flor film 83
Florita dry flor 43
flor sherry 21, 66, 81-84
flor yeast 21, 66, 81-84
Fornachon, John 34
fortifying spirit 21
Four Crown port 21
Four Crown wines 23
Fowler, D. J., Ltd 26
France 67-69, 75, 78, 88, 90, 91
Francis, Les 8
Freiburg 98

107

French oak 36, 56, 69
French vermouth 67
Fromm's Winery 57
Frontignac 31, 58, 59, 72, 86
fructose 74
fused oils 77

G

Galway Fino Sherry 21
Galway, Governor 21
Galway Pipe Port 19, 21
Gamay Beaujolais 71
gas chromatography 77
Gawler 1, 6, 94
Geisenheim 53, 91, 92
gelatin 80
*Gellert* 46
generic names 67, 68
German practices 15
German Rhine Wine Queen 61
German settlement 3
German wine festivals 60
German wines 16
Germany 32, 54, 67, 68, 81, 90
germicide 78
Gewürztraminer 69, 99
Gilbert 22
Glenelg 2
Glen View 49
glucose 74
glycerine 77
Gnadenberg 31
Gnadenfrei 4, 5, 7
Golden Grove 9
Golden Ridge White Wine 22
Gordo Blanco 72
Gramp, Colin 13, 16-18, 61, 65
Gramp, Fred 13
Gramp, G., & Sons Pty Ltd 12
Gramp, Gustav 12
Gramp, Hugo 13
Gramp, Johann, 3, 12, 18, 46
Gramp, Keith 13

Gramp's 5, 47, 57, 65, 82
Gramp, Sid 13
Gramps Orlando 12-18
Grandfather Port 24, 25
granite 97
grape particles 78
grape seed oil 64
grape spirit 71, 81
grape sugar 74
graves 66-68
Great Barossa 54
Greenock 6, 36, 93
Grenache 9, 21, 22, 25, 48, 56, 70, 72, 86, 87, 89
Griffith 8, 64
Gruenberg 4

H

Hackett, Max 64
Hage, Suzanne 61
Hagley, Bob 49
Hahn Dennis 35
Hallett's Valley 47
Hamilton's Ewell Vineyards Pty Ltd 58-9
Hanckel, Norman 22
Hanisch, Arthur 63
Hardy's Siegersdorf 50-51
Hardy, Thomas & Sons 28, 49
Hardy, Tom 13
Harslevelü 69
Haselgrove, Colin 26
Hawker, Charles 13
Heath, Richard, 49, 50
Hebart, Armin 52
Henschke 31-33
Henschke, C. A., & Co. 31
Henschke, Cyril 31, 32
Henschke, Doris 32
Henschke, Johann Christian 31, 32
Henschke, Paul 32
Henschke, Paul Alfred 32

108

Henschke, Stephen 32
Hermitage 31, 52, 59, 70
Hickinbotham, Ian 36
higher acid 67
Hill of Grace 31-33
Hill-Smith, John 20, 61
Hill-Smith, Mark 20
Hill-Smith, Sid 13, 20
Hill-Smith, Wyndham 20
Hindmarsh, Governor 2
Hock 66, 67, 73
Hoffmann, Bruce 46, 60
Hoffmann, Erwin 46
Hoffmann, Gottlieb 42
Hoffmann, Laurel, M.B.E. 46, 61
Hoffmann's 46
Hoffmann, Samuel 3, 46
Hofnungstal 34
homoclimes 90
Hood, Bryce 37
Hope Valley 63
Hunter River 68, 69, 88
Hunter River Riesling 68, 88
Hunter wines 62
hydrated aluminium silicate 78
hydrometer 75

I

Imperial Tokay 69
Individual Vineyard wines 36
ion-exchange 79
Irvine, Jim 49, 50
Italian vermouth 67
Italy 23

J

Jacob's Creek 3, 12, 18, 65
Jenkinson, Oliver 22
Jenkins, Ross 11
Jerez 82
Jerez-de-la-Frontera 82
Jolly, Tim 26
Jutschlau 31

K

Kabminye 5, 49
Kaesler, Mostyn 43
Kaiser Stuhl 5, 34-38, 39, 61, 64
Kalimna 26
Kangaroo Creek Reservoir 5
Kapunda 3
Karrawirra winery 63
Kavel, Pastor August Ludwig Christian 3
Kelly's Cellar 64
Kelly, Ted 57
Kersbrook 5
Keyneton 31, 32, 94
Kidd, Ray 42
Kies, Ken 63
Klemzig 9
Klosterneuberg 20, 37
Kluczko, Tony 16
Kolarovich, George 34, 36, 37, 60
Kraehenbuhl, Dean 57
Kronberger, Rudi 20, 29
Krondorf 5
Kulmbach 12
"Kyeema" air disaster 12, 20

L

lactic acid 77
Laffer, Phillip 42
Lake, Max 22, 62
Langhorne Creek 29, 30
Langmeil 3-5
large wood 70
Lawson, Charles 17
Lehmann, Peter 29, 30, 60, 62
Lehmann, Waldemar 57
Liebfraumilch 43
Liebich, B. & Sons 52
Liebich, Benno Paul 52
Liebich, C. W. 52
Liebich, H. K. 52
Liedertafel 4
Light, Colonel William 2, 3

Light's Pass 94
Lindeman's Wines Ltd 42
Lindner, Bill 47
Lindner, Carl 47
Lindner, Elmore 47
Litchfield, Robert 34
Loder, Max 98
low acid 67
Ludlow, Fred 29
Lyndoch 1, 2, 5, 6, 34, 35, 53, 56, 63, 64, 93, 94, 97
Lynedoch, Lord 2

M

Mac 4-stage press 15
madeira 66, 69, 72, 87, 88
Magill 24, 26
Malbec 58, 86, 87, 89
malic acid 74
Mamre Brook 28
Marananga 5, 7
marc 64
Marchant, Murray 58
Marion 58
marsala 66
marsala all'uovo 35
Martin, Henry 30
Martin, H. M., & Son Pty Ltd 29
Martini & Rossi 23
mass spectroscopy 77
Matara 49
Mataro 9, 22, 72, 86, 89
Materne, A. E. 36
maturation 36
McLaren Vale 49
McNeil, John 39
Mediterranean climate 90
Medlands Estate 63
Médoc 70
Menge, Johann 2, 3
Menglers Hill 5
merlot 99
metatartaric acid 80

Miamba Claret 16
Miamba Riesling Hock 16
micaceous schist 97
Milbrook Reservoir 5
Mildura 100
Mile End 49
minerals 77
Montmorillon 78
montmorillonite 78
Morrastel 86
Morris, Daphne 61
Morris, Tom 61
Mosel 68, 90
moselle 16, 59, 66-68
Mosel Valley 18
Mt Dandenong 12
Mt Edelstein 31
Mt Edelstone 31
Mt Kitchener 5, 35
Mt Lofty Ranges 1, 35
Munich University 37
Murray Irrigation Scheme 20, 88
Murray River 2, 64, 88, 89
Murray Valley 18
Murrumbidgee 88
muscadelle 69
muscat 5, 7, 66, 72, 79
muscatelle 72
Muscat de Frontignan 72
Muscat Gordo Blanco 69, 84, 86, 89

N

national dancing groups 60
Neuschlesien 3
nevers 36
New Silesia 3
Nicholls, Frank 65
Nilsson, Gordon 39
nitrogen 80
noble rot 15
North Para 1, 3, 9, 41, 46, 52, 53, 96

INDEX

North Para Wines Pty Ltd 46
Nuriootpa 1, 3-6, 24-26, 34, 39, 41, 49, 61, 63, 64, 91, 92, 94, 98, 99
Nuriootpa Viticultural Research Station 99

O
oak casks 72, 80, 81, 83
Obst, Stan 64
Oeillade 86
off-flavours 75
Oliver's Blend 22
oloroso 21, 43, 84
Orlando 12-18, 64
oxidation 78, 80, 82

P
Palomino 21, 82, 87
Paradale winery 63
Para Liqueur 9
Parsons, G. A. 22
Pearl wines 14, 66, 71
Pedro 21
Pedro Ximenes 82, 87
Pedro Ximenes Oloroso Sherry 47
Penfold's 24-27, 58
Penfolds Wines Pty Ltd 24-27
Penrice 3
Percy's Blend 22
pests 98
Petite Sirah 70
Petras, J. F. W. 63
Pewsey Vale 19, 22, 94
Pewsey Vale Park 94
Pewsey Vale Rhine Riesling 22
Pewsey Vale Station 22
Pfeiffer, Harold 16
photosynthesis 74
*Phylloxera* 85
Pinot Noir 71, 99
pipe 22
pneumatic press 42

podzol 97
Poland 35
pomace 64
port 24-29, 66, 71
Port Gawler 1
Portugal (grape variety) 87
Portugal 21, 90
potassium bitartrate 64, 79
*pourriture noble* 15
Prass, Günter 16
Prescott, Professor 90
pressurator 15
pressure tanks 37, 57
Prince, Ron 42
Private Bin Port 56
Private Bins 43
product recovery 64
propyl alcohol 77
pruning 98, 100

Q
Qantas 61
quality control 37

R
racking 78, 80
Radford, Reg 98
rainfall 91
Ramco 18
Ramsay, Michael 26
Rankin, Reg 64
Rayner, William 58
Reckitt & Colman Ltd 17
red-brown earths 96
red table wines 66, 69-71
refractometer 75
Reim, Heidrun 61
relative humidity 91
rendzina 97
research 98-101
Reserve Bins 43
Reynella 63
Reynell, Walter, & Sons Pty Ltd 63

Rex, Bob 64
Rheingau 92
Rheinland 92
Rhine 35, 53, 68, 87, 90, 91
Rhine Riesling 29, 30, 50, 52, 54, 56, 59, 68, 87, 89
Rhone Valley 70
Riesling 14, 16, 22, 31, 35, 36, 43, 45, 50, 51, 58, 66, 68, 69, 74, 87
Rinegolde 41, 42
Riverina 68
Rogers, W. C. & R. V. 36
rosé 35, 66, 70
Roseworthy Agricultural College 26, 37, 56, 99
Rovalley Wines 52
Rowland 3
Rowland Flat 3, 5, 17, 18, 47, 52, 65
Royal Agricultural Societies 36
Royal Reserve Port 21, 25
ruby port 66, 71, 72
Rutherglen 8, 10, 11

S

*Saccharomyces* 83, 84
Salt Creek 85
Salter, Edward 3, 28
Salter, Leslie 28
Salter, William 3, 28
Saltram 28-30
Samuel's Blend 22
Sandy Creek 6
sauterne 66-68
Sauvignon Blanc 5, 72
Schiller wine 54
schloss 53
Schoenbron 5
Scholz, P. A. 26
Schroeter, Kevin 26
Schroeter, Les 26
Schutz, Norm 26

Seat of Kings 34
*sec* 71
Second World War 58
Seitz factory 16
Sekt 54, 66
Seppelt, Benno 9, 10
Seppelt, Bill 11
Seppelt, Bill Jnr 11
Seppelt, Graham 11
Seppelt, Ian 9, 10
Seppelt, J. G. 7
Seppelt, John 10
Seppelt, Joseph Ernst 3, 9, 11
Seppelt, Karl 11
Seppelt, Leo 10, 11
Seppelt, Malcolm 9, 11
Seppelt, Nicholas 11
Seppelt, Oscar 10, 58
Seppelt's 5, 7-11, 82
Seppelt's 1895 Barossa Port 62
Seppeltsfield 3, 5, 7-11, 63, 93
Seppelt, Waldemar 10
Sémillon 16, 30, 31, 68, 87-89
Semmler, Oscar 34
Sercial 31, 87
service company 64
Shea Oak Log 6
Sheppard, Frank 62
sherry 21, 66, 67, 81, 86
Shipster, Reg 41-44
Shiraz 9, 17, 21, 22, 25, 28-31, 36, 45, 48, 52, 56, 58, 59, 69, 70, 71, 87, 89
Shiraz Mataro Claret 46
Show Port 21
Sidney's Blend 22
Siegersdorf 5, 49-51
Siegersdorf Rhine Riesling 50
Silesia 3, 31, 35, 47
Silesian dialect 4
*Skjold* 32
Smith, Derek 89
Smith, Percival 20

# INDEX

Smith, S. & Sons 19
Smith, Samuel 3, 19
Smith, Sidney 19, 20
Smith, Walter 20
Smyth, Jim 37
Sobels, Kevin 9
soils 96-97, 101
solar radiation 91
solera system 29
solodized solonetz 96, 97
South African sherry 82
South Australian Company 3
Southern Vales 22
South Para River 1
Spain 82
Spanish sherry 82
sparkling burgundy 66, 71
sparkling hock 66, 71
sparkling moselle 66, 71
sparkling pearl wines 14
sparkling wines 66, 71
spätlese 15, 16, 59, 74
spectrophotometry 77
spirit recovery 64
Springton 1, 50, 57, 94, 97
Springton Riesling 58, 59
Star Wine 12, 13
Steingarten 18
Steingarten Riesling 18
St Emillon 69
Stephens, Eric 36
St Hallett's Wines 47-8, 57
Stirling 6
St Kitt's Hills 1
Stonyfell 29
Stonyfell Vineyards 29
Sturt Highway 6, 35, 45, 52, 53, 63
St Vincent's Gulf 1
succinic acid 77
sucrose 74
sugar 67, 74, 77
sugar phosphate ester 76

sulphur dioxide 13, 76, 78, 81, 82
sultana grapes 100
Sunraysia 100
sweet sherry 11, 84
Sylvaner 66, 99
Syrah 70

T

T.A.A. 61
Tabor 4
tails 77
tannin 70, 84
Tanunda 1, 3-5, 9, 24, 32, 41, 45, 49, 61, 63, 65, 94
Tanunda Creek 2
Tanunda Liedertafel 4, 61
Tarac 64
tartaric acid 74
tawny port 66, 70-72
Temperano 21
temperature 91
terra rossa 97
Thumm, Dieter 53
Thumm, Hermann 53-55, 64
Thumm, Robert 53
Tintara 26
titratable acidity 75
Tokay, 16, 21, 30, 66, 69, 72, 87
Tolley, Douglas A., Pty Ltd 63
Tolley, Scott & Tolley Ltd 27, 39-46
Torrens Gorge 5
tourism 64, 102
trace elements 76
Trebbiano 69, 87
trellising 98
*Trockenbeeren auslese* 16
tronçais 36
T.S.T. brandy 39
Tulloch, Harry 98
Tummel, Mark 16
Tummel, Phil 40
Turin 23

## U

Ugni Blanc 31, 69, 87
ullage 83
underground water 94
United States 71, 78
University of Adelaide 26, 37, 53, 54, 89

## V

varietal name 68
verdelho 69
Veritas Winery 63
vermouth 23, 35, 66, 67
Vickery, John 41, 43
Vienna 20, 37
Village Fair 61
vine bud mite 98
vinegar bacteria 83
Vine Inn 65
Vine Vale 50, 97
Vineyards Motel 83
Vin-spa 57
Vintage Ball 61
Vintage Claret 54
Vintage Festival 60-62
Vintage Port 66, 71, 72
Vintage Tawny Port 17
Vintage Queen 61
Vintners Co. Pty Ltd 20, 64
Virgo, Jeff 16
Vitamin C 80
*Vitis* 2, 85
*Vitis vinifera* 85

## W

Wade, Bob 40
Waikerie 18, 39
Waite Agricultural Research Institute 90
Walker, Ewald 54
Wall, Peter 20
Walter, Robert 54
Ward, Ray 20
Wark, Alf 20
Warren, Roger 26, 49, 50
Waterman, Keith 61
water stress 95
Watervale 43
Watson Prize 45
Weingarten 61
Weinkeller restaurant 65
West Germany 53, 61, 90, 92
Whispering Wall 6
White burgundy 66, 67
White Frontignac 69
White Hermitage 69, 87
White Muscat 72
white of egg 80
White Shiraz 69, 87
white table wines 66–69
Williamstown 1, 5, 6, 94
Wilsford Wines 56
Wilson, Neville 37
wind 91
Wine & Brandy Producers Association of S.A. 11
Wine & Brandy Producers Council of Australia 10
Wine Auction 61
*Wine Cookery* 20
winemaking processes 77–81
wine types 66–72
Wine Week 13
Woodside 6
Wustewaltersdorf 9
Wyncroft 36

## Y

Yaldara 53
Yalumba 3, 19-23, 30, 82
Yalumba 1929 Claret 62
yeast 74, 76-78, 80, 82-84
Yugoslavia 37

## Z

Zugspitze Birnenwein 30